EYE ON
Art

MEDIEVAL EUROPEAN ART AND ARCHITECTURE

by Don Nardo

LUCENT BOOKS
A part of Gale, Cengage Learning

GALE
CENGAGE Learning·

Detroit • New York • San Francisco • New Haven, Conn • Waterville, Maine • London

LIBRARY OF CONGRESS CATALOGING-IN-PUBLICATION DATA

Nardo, Don, 1947-
  Medieval European art and architecture / by Don Nardo.
      p. cm. -- (Eye on art)
  Includes bibliographical references and index.
  ISBN 978-1-4205-0715-7 (hardcover)
  1. Art, Medieval--Juvenile literature. 2. Architecture, Medieval--Juvenile literature. I. Title.
  N5970.N37 2012
  709.02--dc23
                                                                2011032811

Lucent Books
27500 Drake Rd
Farmington Hills MI 48331

ISBN-13: 978-1-4205-0715-7
ISBN-10: 1-4205-0715-X

Printed in the United States of America
1 2 3 4 5 6 7 15 14 13 12 11

CONTENTS

Foreword. 5

Introduction 8
   For the Glory of God

Chapter 1 14
   Castles and Other Secular Architecture

Chapter 2 28
   Churches and Other Religious Structures

Chapter 3 44
   Sculpture: Romanesque to Renaissance

Chapter 4 58
   Evolving Painting Forms and Techniques

Chapter 5 73
   Mosaics and Stained Glass: A Dual Role

Chapter 6 85
   Tapestry, Jewelry, and Other Fine Crafts

Notes 99

Glossary 102

For More Information 104

Index. 107

Picture Credits 112

About the Author. 112

Foreword

"Art has no other purpose than to brush aside . . . everything that veils reality from us in order to bring us face to face with reality itself."

—French philosopher Henri-Louis Bergson

Some thirty-one thousand years ago, early humans painted strikingly sophisticated images of horses, bison, rhinoceroses, bears, and other animals on the walls of a cave in southern France. The meaning of these elaborate pictures is unknown, although some experts speculate that they held ceremonial significance. Regardless of their intended purpose, the Chauvet-Pont-d'Arc cave paintings represent some of the first known expressions of the artistic impulse.

From the Paleolithic era to the present day, human beings have continued to create works of visual art. Artists have developed painting, drawing, sculpture, engraving, and many other techniques to produce visual representations of landscapes, the human form, religious and historical events, and countless other subjects. The artistic impulse also finds expression in glass, jewelry, and new forms inspired by new technology. Indeed, judging by humanity's prolific artistic output throughout history, one must conclude that the compulsion to produce art is an inherent aspect of being human, and the results are among humanity's greatest cultural achievements: masterpieces such as the architectural marvels of ancient Greece, Michelangelo's perfectly rendered statue *David*, Vincent van Gogh's visionary painting *Starry Night*, and endless other treasures.

The creative impulse serves many purposes for society. At its most basic level, art is a form of entertainment or the means for a satisfying or pleasant aesthetic experience. But art's true power lies not in its potential to entertain and delight but in its ability to enlighten, to reveal the truth, and by doing so to uplift the human spirit and transform the human race.

One of the primary functions of art has been to serve religion. For most of Western history, for example, artists were paid by the church to produce works with religious themes and subjects. Art was thus a tool to help human beings transcend mundane, secular reality and achieve spiritual enlightenment. One of the best-known, and largest-scale, examples of Christian religious art is the Sistine Chapel in the Vatican in Rome. In 1508 Pope Julius II commissioned Italian Renaissance artist Michelangelo to paint the chapel's vaulted ceiling, an area of 640 square yards (535 sq. m). Michelangelo spent four years on scaffolding, his neck craned, creating a panoramic fresco of some three hundred human figures. His paintings depict Old Testament prophets and heroes, sibyls of Greek mythology, and nine scenes from the Book of Genesis, including the Creation of Adam, the Fall of Adam and Eve from the Garden of Eden, and the Flood. The ceiling of the Sistine Chapel is considered one of the greatest works of Western art and has inspired the awe of countless Christian pilgrims and other religious seekers. As eighteenth-century German poet and author Johann Wolfgang von Goethe wrote, "Until you have seen this Sistine Chapel, you can have no adequate conception of what man is capable of."

In addition to inspiring religious fervor, art can serve as a force for social change. Artists are among the visionaries of any culture. As such, they often perceive injustice and wrongdoing and confront others by reflecting what they see in their work. One classic example of art as social commentary was created in May 1937, during the brutal Spanish civil war. On May 1 Spanish artist Pablo Picasso learned of the recent attack on the small Basque village of Guernica by German airplanes allied with fascist forces led by Francisco Franco. The German pilots had used the village for target practice, a three-hour bombing that killed sixteen hundred civilians. Picasso, living in Paris, channeled his outrage over the massacre into his painting *Guernica,* a black, white, and gray mural that depicts dismembered animals and fractured human figures whose faces are contorted in agonized expressions. Initially, critics and the public condemned the painting as an incoherent hodgepodge, but the work soon came to be seen as a powerful antiwar statement and remains an iconic symbol of the violence and terror that dominated world events during the remainder of the twentieth century.

The impulse to create art—whether painting animals with crude pigments on a cave wall, sculpting a human form from marble, or commemorating human tragedy in a mural—thus serves many purposes. It offers an entertaining diversion, nourishes the imagination and the spirit, decorates and beautifies the world, and chronicles the age. But underlying all these functions is the desire to reveal that which is obscure— to illuminate, clarify, and perhaps ennoble. As Picasso himself stated, "The purpose of art is washing the dust of daily life off our souls."

The Eye on Art series is intended to assist readers in understanding the various roles of art in society. Each volume offers an in-depth exploration of a major artistic movement, medium, figure, or profession. All books in the series are beautifully illustrated with full-color photographs and diagrams. Riveting narrative, clear technical explanation, informative sidebars, fully documented quotes, a bibliography, and a thorough index all provide excellent starting points for research and discussion. With these features, the Eye on Art series is a useful introduction to the world of art—a world that can offer both insight and inspiration.

For the Glory of God

"Your art is, as it were, God's grandchild."[1] So the dead Roman poet Virgil tells the living Italian poet Dante during the latter's imaginary visit to hell in the classic fourteenth-century work *The Divine Comedy*. By "your art," Virgil means the art of Dante's era, today referred to as either medieval times or the Middle Ages. The term *medieval* derives from the Latin phrase *medium aevum*, meaning "the age in the middle." Historians define it as the period lying between, or in the middle of, ancient times and modern times and date it from about A.D. 500 to 1500 or somewhat later.

When the reanimated Virgil calls medieval art "God's grandchild," he means to say two interrelated things. First, artists are endowed with their talents by God and so they are deeply beholden to their creator. Second, Virgil verbalizes a common belief of the Middle Ages—that true art is inspired by God and should be aimed at venerating him. As the late British art critic and historian Anne Fremantle put it, medieval artists fashioned

> works of superb beauty not "for art's sake" . . . but chiefly for the greater glory of God. The master builder [architect] dedicated himself to erecting a house of the Lord. Sculptors, painters, mosaicists [makers of mosaics], goldsmiths, silversmiths, and inspired craftsmen

working in wood, glass, and stone dedicated themselves to adorning it. Musicians composed [tunes] to enhance the rites of worship which the Lord's house sheltered. The skills were diverse, but all art had the same aim—to express . . . the glory of the Creator.[2]

Some Arts Better than Others?

True, medieval artists were partly motivated by the need to make a living and were accordingly paid for doing their work. But having taken on a job, even if it did not involve building or decorating a church, they strongly believed that God was watching them. Almost everyone in Europe during the Middle Ages was devoutly religious. It was drilled into them from an early age that God was everywhere at once and knew not only what people did, but even what they were thinking. Therefore, to strive for excellence for God's sake was almost a given for an artist. Although some modern art is still inspired by a god or gods and intended to exalt them, the majority of today's artists pursue their creative instincts for secular, or non-religious, reasons. Most medieval artists would have viewed this as unusual, odd, or even disturbing.

There were other ways in which medieval people viewed the arts differently than they are commonly seen today. First, some artistic pursuits were deemed better, or more virtuous and worthwhile—or even more moral—than others. For instance, gold was widely viewed as the most noble material in existence. So creating gold figurines, jewelry, or other objects was seen as a worthy endeavor and profession. In contrast, bronze was viewed as less noble than gold; hence, an artisan who worked with bronze was engaged in a less admirable occupation.

As for painting and sculpture, a vigorous debate raged among thinkers, artists, and others during the 1400s and 1500s over which pursuit was better. Eminent museum scholars Glyn Davies and Kirstin Kennedy explain:

Painting was arguably better than sculpture because its use of color offered the most realistic way of recording the natural world. [Other] scholars had a different agenda: to argue that the use of color elevated the status of the practitioner [artist] from mechanical craftsman to skilled intellectual. Fifteenth-century writers such as the Italian scholar Poliziano drew on arguments marshaled by [ancient writers] to argue that painters could use color to depict landscapes, the weather, a person's expression, or the vivid effects of light and shade. In short, painting illuminated "hidden things," whereas sculpture did not, and could not.[3]

Madonna Enthroned by medieval Italian artist Giotto di Bondone is representative of the strong religious influences in medieval art.

Religious Restrictions on Artists

Likewise, for a long time medieval society did not routinely respect and honor its artists. Instead they were seen as mere artisans, or skilled workers, who manipulated various materials to create objects of varying value. In general, the more that manual work was involved in making those objects, the less worthy the profession and the artisan were perceived to be.

On the flip side, the more intellectual and/or spiritual involvement there was in the creation of an object, the more worthwhile and commendable the work and artisan. For this reason, an architect who designed a building in his head and/or on paper was seen as superior to the people who sweated and dirtied their hands in the actual construction of the building. These views, art historian Janetta R. Benton explains, were "linked to the medieval disdain for manual work as . . . inferior to spiritual pursuits, and the active life as less desirable than the contemplative [intellectual] life—[in other words] work of the hands was less valued than that of the mind."[4] Once again, therefore, spiritual concerns outweighed all others.

In addition to working in what society saw as decidedly less-than-admirable occupations, most medieval artists were not allowed the high degree of individuality, originality, and inventiveness that modern artists enjoy. "Only on exceptional occasions did a medieval artist have significant artistic liberty," Benton makes clear.

> Individuality was not valued in the medieval way of thinking, and an artist's personal style was neither cultivated nor encouraged. The quest for innovation, the desire to do something new, the belief that novelty is inherently good, are all ideas that had little place in medieval art and, in fact, were discouraged until the last years of the Middle Ages. The concept of an art school or art academy in which individuals are educated . . . so that they might realize their potential by developing their own aesthetic [artistic sense] was many years in the future.[5]

Moreover, the majority of artists in the Middle Ages almost never had the luxury of choosing the subjects and themes of their artworks. In most cases the subject and even the general look of an artwork was dictated by the customer who hired the artist. That customer was often the Christian Church, which commissioned a hefty portion of medieval art. In fact, with few exceptions the builders, painters, sculptors, and other artists employed by churches had to follow traditional guidelines supplied by bishops and other clergy. It was expected that such workers would adhere to a general rule created by a meeting of influential bishops in the eighth century. "The composition of religious imagery," it stated, "is not left to the initiative of the artists, but is formed upon principles laid down by the Catholic Church and by religious tradition."[6]

The serious nature of such religious restrictions on artists was illustrated by an incident that occurred in England in 1306. A German-born artisan named Tidemann was paid to carve a crucifix for a London church and took the creative liberty of rendering a few details differently than in traditional versions. Angry

In medieval times, the greater the intellectual and/or spiritual involvement in the creation of an object, the more valued it was. Architects, for example, were seen as superior to the workmen who constructed the buildings.

church authorities said that the object was "quite contrary to the true representation of the cross" and that the very sight of it by local worshippers would cause "peril for their souls."[7] The bishop forced Tidemann to give back the money he had been paid for the work and to immediately take the offending object outside the limits of the diocese (local Catholic district).

Most Artists' Names Lost

One unfortunate side effect of such lack of respect for and restrictions on artists was damage to their pride. In society's eyes they were at best mundane workers who possessed little originality, followed strict tradition, and mostly did what they were told. So most of the people who came into possession of artworks had little or no interest in knowing who made them. Under these sad circumstances, there was no compelling reason for an artist to sign his work, a custom that is universal among modern artists. Indeed, as one modern expert points out, the medieval era witnessed a "scarcity of signatures on works of art, as well as [a] scarcity of portraits and self-portraits."[8]

There were some obvious exceptions to the anonymity of medieval artists. In the last few centuries of the era, the builders of major structures, such as cathedrals, were well known to both those who hired them and the citizens of the towns where such structures were located. The identities of the sculptors and painters who worked on those buildings were also known to the locals. A major reason that the names of most of those talented individuals are obscure or unknown today is that no one in their day thought it was important to record their names in writing. As a result, their names were lost over time.

Even though the names of most of the architects and other artists did not endure, their artworks quite often did. From intricate paintings to imposing statues, and from ornate tapestries and book illustrations to soaring cathedrals, these often stunning artworks, most of them deeply inspired by their makers' love for God, live on. In Fremantle's words, "they survive, splendid still, in Europe today, a testament to [people's] capacity to infuse [their] artistic achievements with [their] faith."[9]

Castles and Other Secular Architecture

After more than a century of invasions by tribal peoples from northern Europe, the western Roman Empire disintegrated in the fifth and sixth centuries. At that point the creation of large-scale buildings, at which the Romans had excelled, temporarily ceased across Europe. The main reason was a widespread lack of proper organizational and economic abilities. Put simply, the scattered small kingdoms the invaders built upon Rome's wreckage were poorly organized and had neither the money nor the will to create monumental, or large-scale, art.

Indeed, of all the arts, architecture produces by far the largest individual artistic objects. A cathedral takes much longer and is much more costly to create than a statue, a painting, or a piece of fine furniture. Major commitments of money, time, and people are required to build immense, highly decorated structures like palaces, cathedrals, castles, and stately domes. Such commitments did not come about in Europe in a significant way until the beginning of the Central, or High, Middle Ages, dated by historians from roughly 1000 to 1300.

Before that, medieval Europeans lived in houses made primarily of perishable materials like wood and thatch (bundled tree branches). Even larger structures, such as forts, were made of these substances, and little or no thought went into their aesthetic, or artistic, qualities. As the Central Middle Ages progressed, however, historian Judith M. Bennett explains, "stone churches, abbeys, castles, hospitals, and town halls were built in prodigious numbers. More stone was quarried in central medieval France alone than by pyramid and temple builders in the 3,000-year history of ancient Egypt. The most celebrated buildings of the [age] are great and awesome . . . [and were] built with skill and [are] still beautiful today."[10]

The structures Bennett lists fall into two broad categories of architecture—religious (nonsecular) or nonreligious (secular). At first, most of the secular architecture revolved around castles and other fortified structures built for defense. But as time went on, ornate private mansions and numerous town squares, town halls, and other public buildings appeared. Most were intended by their makers to have visual appeal and to that end were adorned with fancy porches, gates, and windows, along with sculptures and other decorations.

The Visual Appeal of Castles

The largest and usually the most imposing secular medieval structures were castles. In modern eyes they have become the architectural trademarks, so to speak, of Europe in that era. Their brooding stone towers, battlements, and drawbridges routinely conjure up images of chivalrous knights in armor, rich lords exploiting poor peasants, and sieges with catapults hurling huge rocks at and over towering stone walls.

Several modern books dealing with medieval art have excluded castles from the discussion, arguing that these were military constructions with no aesthetic values. But most major art historians disagree. Although castles were meant to provide security for their inhabitants, one scholar points out, their builders took care to make them look well-proportioned and visually impressive. "Medieval secular architecture emphasized visual appeal, often at the expense of comfort and convenience. This was true of dwellings ranging from modest half-timbered constructions to lavish manor houses. Castles and fortresses

In the beginning of the medieval period, most secular architecture was devoted to castles and other fortified structures built for defense.

were built with an interest not only in defense, but also in aesthetics."[11]

Nicola Coldstream, one of the leading experts on medieval architecture, agrees. The masons and carpenters of that era, she says, "did not specialize in particular building types, but were equally responsible for all of them." Moreover, "the same methods were used to [build] castles and churches, with the same care for planning, shaping interior space, and outward show. . . . Architecture was about ritual and display, a backdrop for ceremonial [activities], from dinner [parties] to celebrating church festivals [to] the display of power."[12]

Castle Evolution

Contrary to popular assumptions, this display of power, along with the images of romantic chivalry that large stone castles generated, did not exist in the early medieval centuries. Stone castles did not appear in Europe until shortly after the year 1000. Moreover, full-blown versions with multiple towers, gates, and courtyards took another century or two to develop.

When wealthy lords began to build stone castles in Europe, the basic architectural concepts were not new. Indeed, the ancient Romans had constructed numerous large-scale stone forts across Europe and North Africa. Even these structures had not been original, because various Middle Eastern peoples had erected such fortresses in the ages before Rome's rise. Nevertheless, medieval Europeans took the art of stone castle building to new heights by using architectural layouts and decorative touches that made these structures blend perfectly with the more ornate cathedrals and churches that grew up around them.

The first medieval European castles appeared in northern France in the late 800s and early 900s. Called motte-and-bailey castles, they were made mostly of wood and consisted of a

A HUMBLE MONK-ARTIST

One of the earliest medieval artists who left behind a likeness of himself was Airardus, who worked on the original Basilica of Saint-Denis, erected in the late 700s a few miles north of Paris, France. A Benedictine monk, he created the bronze doors for what was then a Romanesque-like structure. (A few centuries later, another churchman, Abbot Suger, renovated it, turning it into a Gothic cathedral.) The sculpted image of Airardus that appeared on the doors showed a man with a round, plump face wearing the ankle-length robes then typical for monks. He added an accompanying inscription in Latin in which he humbly dedicated his doors to Saint Denis.

primitive two- or three-story tower surrounded by a tall stockade barrier. This fortification stood on a low hill, called the motte. One or more baileys, large courtyards that were also protected by wooden stockades, nestled at the base of the hill. When the locals were under attack, they took refuge in the baileys, while their rich lord and his soldiers defended the fort atop the motte.

Beginning in the late eleventh century, virtually all of the motte and baileys were rapidly replaced by castles featuring sturdier, more durable stone walls. Large-scale defensive features were added. These included the familiar-looking crenellation—alternating stone notches and open spaces—along the tops of the walls and towers. When under attack, soldiers hid behind the notches and fired arrows through the open spaces. Other major protective features included tall guard towers; huge gates with drawbridges; and machicolation, which was the outward projection of a wall at the top of a battlement (so that rocks or boiling oil could be dropped onto attackers through openings in the bottom of the projection).

The ruined structure seen here was originally an updated, refurbished version of a motte-and-bailey castle, in which the wooden stockades were replaced by stone walls.

Celebrating "Castleness"

Castles continued to develop, becoming larger and more complex in the process. Stone castles also became vehicles for the owners to show off their wealth and sophistication. They had "both a military and a political function," art historian Marilyn Stokstad points out, "and established an aura of power and wealth for a family."[13] Architecturally speaking, such structures retained what Coldstream calls "the symbolism of warfare," as they were "decked out" in the "detail of towers, gatehouses, moats, and drawbridges." Yet as time went on, defensive features were more and more combined with artistic details and touches that signaled the wealth and power of the lords who lived in these structures. "Castle-builders began to celebrate an idea of 'castleness,' while tricking them out in ornament,"[14] Coldstream says. Examples of such decoration included statues or elegant pointed pinnacles atop the crenellated notches, sculpted animals and/or faces of lords or kings above the main gates, relief sculptures on the towers, elaborate tapestries on the interior walls, and glass windows bordered by intricately carved moldings.

At the same time, certain artistic castle features began to be applied to other types of structures, such as large manor houses, palaces, town halls, and university buildings. A good example is the great town hall at Siena, Italy, which was built in the thirteenth century and survives today. It features simulated crenellation along its roof fronts and a tall tower made of brick faced with stone.

Most typical, however, were gatehouses built on the grounds of palaces, university buildings, and other major secular structures. Such gatehouses usually had towers, or turrets, on either side of the central opening, miniature crenellation and/or machicolation, and carefully carved decorative features. More than most examples of this castle-inspired architecture, Coldstream writes, "Queens' College, Cambridge [in England], set a fashion for turreted gatehouses." Its architectural decorations were an obvious and well-executed version "of their source, the castle of the thirteenth century."[15]

The design of this thirteenth-century town hall in Siena, Italy, incorporates architectural details more typically seen in castles.

Reviving Classical Architecture

The architecture of structures such as town halls and other public buildings underwent a new burst of inspiration and energetic construction in the final phase of Europe's medieval period —the Renaissance. This pivotal era lasted from about 1400 to 1600 for large-scale architecture. "Renaissance means 'rebirth,'" noted art historian Roy Bolton says. "And by the fourteenth century this is exactly what artists began to think themselves a part of—the [symbolic or artistic] rebirth of the Greco-Roman world. They were self-consciously rebuilding everything the Ancients stood for, from architecture and science to sculpture."[16]

Scholars of the early Renaissance, especially a group called the humanists, were profoundly inspired by recently rediscovered

THE HUMANISTS

*A*mong the intellectual guiding forces behind the cultural and artistic period known as the Renaissance was a group of talented, influential thinkers and artists who came to call themselves humanists (from the Latin word *humanitas*, meaning "humanity"). The most prominent humanists included Italy's Francesco Petrarch (born 1304) and Giovanni Boccaccio (born 1313), Netherlands' Desiderius Erasmus (born 1466), France's François Rabelais (born 1495), and England's Thomas More (born 1478).

Most of these men were devoutly religious. Yet they felt that God had given humans the gifts of intelligence and curiosity. With these abilities, they believed, it was only natural for people to search for and hopefully find the truths of life and the universe. The key tools in this quest were held to be reason and logic. The humanists also wanted to use any newfound knowledge to enrich society as well as glorify God. This was particularly true of the "civic" humanists, among whose goals was beautifying the cities in which they lived. One of the outstanding civic humanists was the Floren-

tine Leon Battista Alberti (1404), who designed a number of impressive structures. He was also a poet, athlete, and musician. His many talents made him one of the original models of the so-called Renaissance man, a person with multiple abilities, especially artistic ones.

Englishman Thomas More was Lord Chancellor of England and a leading member of the humanist movement. Most humanists were devoutly religious.

literary works that had been lost in the West for a number of centuries. These had been written by Aristotle and other ancient Greco-Roman, or classical, thinkers, scientists, mathematicians, and architects. In Stokstad's words, "Architects revived features of classical architecture, including the classical orders [the Doric, Ionic, and Corinthian], and borrowed designs and decorative motifs from the ruins of Roman temples, triumphal arches, and tombs."[17]

The "classical orders" to which Stokstad refers were architectural styles, each based on the main features of their columns. Doric columns have plain slabs in their capitals, or tops. Ionic capitals feature curved scrolls called volutes, and Corinthian capitals have ornate masses of carved leaves.

Renaissance builders used columns and other architectural elements based on these orders, or composites of them, on the exteriors of many of their buildings. A brilliant example is the facade, or outside front, of the Palazzo Rucellai, in Florence, Italy. Designed by one of the greatest of all Renaissance architects, Leon Battista Alberti (al-BEAR-tee, born 1404), it was completed in 1451. Alberti placed rows of graceful arches, with columns and pilasters (half columns with flat backs attached to walls) between them, on the exterior of each of the building's three oversized stories. He also encased the windows on the upper two stories in arches and classical pilasters.

In addition, Alberti and his contemporaries used classical pillars in the interiors of their buildings. These columns were usually load bearing, or intended to support the weight of the stories and roofs above them. But Renaissance architects also employed non-load-bearing pilasters as added decoration. Along with frescoes (paintings done on wet plaster), intricately carved moldings, and other decorative effects, Greco-Roman columns and pilasters made the interiors of large-scale Renaissance structures look quite lavish and luxurious.

Immense Inner Spaces

Renaissance architects particularly admired another quality of classical buildings, especially the huge theaters, bathhouses, and basilicas (meeting halls) of ancient Rome. That quality was their immense, visually stunning inner spaces. Some of the larger Roman bathhouses, for instance, had enormous foyers or central rooms. Typical was the central chamber of the Baths of Caracalla, measuring 183 feet (56m) long by 79 feet (24m) wide with a ceiling soaring to a whopping 108 feet (33m). More than seventeen centuries later, the remains of this structure inspired the design of Pennsylvania Station in New York City.

Such colossal ancient Roman structures also motivated Renaissance architects to build both religious and secular edifices on a grand scale. An early secular example was Westminster Hall, in London, erected between 1397 and 1399. Its impressive central

The central space of London's Westminster Hall is an impressive 290 feet long, 68 feet wide, and 92 feet high.

space measures 290 feet (89m) long, 68 feet (21m) wide, and 92 feet (28m) high. Similar large interiors were achieved in the pope's audience hall in Avignon, France, begun in 1335, and the hospital at Tonnerre, France, finished somewhat earlier. One modern expert calls the revival of using such large interior architectural spaces "the greatest achievement of Renaissance architecture."[18]

Renaissance builders also elaborated on classical principles such as balance, proportion, and symmetry. In Italy, Alberti concluded that these qualities were based on sound mathematical ratios expressed in whole numbers, such as 1 to 2, 1 to 3, or 2 to 4. For example, he said, some structures were best laid out in a 1 to 2 ratio, so that their length was twice their width (or, expressed in a different way, their width was half their length). Similarly, the facades of some buildings were best built to reflect other mathematical ratios. The reason that such ratios were best, Alberti believed, was because they were already in a sense embedded in nature, which under the surface was balanced and proportional.

Italian, French, English, and other Renaissance architects incorporated such ratios into their designs, believing they would result in structures of great natural beauty. This was only one item in their architectural toolkit, so to speak. Other items borrowed from classical times included arches, vaults, domes, and columns and pilasters in the three Greco-Roman orders. To these they added numerous decorative elements in styles that had developed during the medieval era, among them carved moldings, statues, marble and tiled floors, stone staircases, windows and window casings, ceilings that were painted or coffered (covered with square-shaped sunken panels), bronze doors, and many others.

The Divine Genius

Typically, Renaissance builders attempted to achieve a measure of originality by mixing these diverse elements in various and innovative combinations. The ultimate goal was to create buildings that were at the same time grand, functional, and

pleasing to the eye. Besides Alberti, a number of Italian architects managed to achieve this goal, including Filippo Brunelleschi (broo-nuh-LESS-kee, born 1377), Giulio Romano (1499), Andrea Palladio (1508), and Giacomo della Porta (1533).

In addition, after about 1500 the Renaissance spread from Italy into several more northerly European countries. At first, large-scale homes, halls, university buildings, and other secular structures in these countries were erected using imported Italian architects. But it did not take long for their talented local counterparts to rise to the task. Among the outstanding native

Work began on Michelangelo's secular masterpiece Piazza Campidoglio in the 1540s but was not completed until decades after the artist's death.

architects in the north in this period were France's Philibert Delorme (1514) and England's Inigo Jones (1573).

According to the consensus of later art historians, the greatest Renaissance architect of all was Michelangelo Buonarroti (bwon-uh-ROT-ee, 1475). Having grown up in Florence, then a great cultural center, as a young man he became a sketch artist, painter, sculptor, and architect of extraordinary talent. In the words of German art historian Elke Linda Buchholz, "Michelangelo was the first artist who was venerated even in his own time as a divine genius." He was also the world's first artist to have biographies written about him while he was still living. As an architect, "he mastered immense formats," including designing huge buildings and even an entire town square, "and lent his [works] grandiose power and clarity"[19] that had never been seen before.

Michelangelo's town square, the Campidoglio, erected on one of Rome's seven hills, was one of his secular architectural masterpieces. (He also designed elements of religious buildings.) Work began on the project in the 1540s and was not completed until several decades after his death. The central section consists of a magnificent oval-shaped plaza roughly half the size of a football field. It is flanked on three sides by government buildings with splendid facades, typically featuring windows encased by ornate columns and arches. Enormous pilasters with Corinthian capitals at their tops separate one window from the next and communicate an intense feeling of strength and majesty. The fourth and front side of the square features the top of a monumental staircase—the Cordonata—which descends to the bottom of the hill.

Michelangelo was no less creative and theatrical in designing *interior* spaces for secular structures. Particularly noteworthy was his entrance hall to the Laurentian Library in Florence, begun in 1524. Here he showed that he was ahead of his time by selecting various classical elements and using them in what were then extremely odd ways. For example, the pilasters on the walls are thinner at the bottoms than at the tops, an effect no other architect had ever employed. Also, the stairs in the central staircase leading to the door are curved instead of rectangular and have progressively unequal widths. It was clear even to Michelangelo's contemporaries that such features were both revolutionary and brilliant. The sixteenth-century Italian painter, architect, and art critic Giorgio Vasari said of the library, "all the building . . . is so unlike the common fashion of [architectural] treatment, that every one stands amazed at the sight [of it]."[20] Nearly five centuries later, people are still amazed when they gaze on Michelangelo's library and other grand secular architectural works created in the final years of Europe's medieval period.

2

Churches and Other Religious Structures

The castles, mansions, town halls, gatehouses, and other striking secular structures erected in the last few medieval centuries were not the only examples of fine architecture. Rather, together they occupied one side of the coin representing the entirety of medieval architecture. On the coin's other side were thousands of churches, chapels, abbeys, and other religious structures built across Europe during the Middle Ages. In general, these buildings employed most of the same architectural features that secular ones did, including arches, vaults, towers, columns, pilasters, domes, carved moldings, and so forth.

What made the religious structures different from the secular ones was that churches were erected specifically to honor God. Christianity had a profound hold on the medieval European mind, and architecture became a potent way to express that deeply held devotion. In Marilyn Stokstad's words, "emperors, kings, popes, and abbots lavished their material resources on churches, altars, and liturgical [ritual-related] equipment in an attempt to glorify God and to re-create an image of the heavenly Jerusalem on earth."[21] The result was the creation of some of history's most beautiful and imposing buildings.

Late Roman and Early Medieval Churches

The earliest large Christian churches in Europe were erected even before Rome's fall. At first they consisted of refurbished Roman basilicas. These huge meeting places featured a spacious central hall called a nave, with long aisles on the sides and a small semicircular space, called an apse, on one or both ends. Eventually, as new churches went up from scratch, architects continued to use the basilica form. In fact, as classical historian Charles Freeman points out, the early Christians felt that

> the basilica model was ideal. The clergy or bishop could be installed at one end [and] large numbers of worshipers could fit inside. The greatest of the [late Roman] basilicas was St. Peter's in Rome, constructed over the shrine which for generations was believed to be the resting place of St. Peter's body. A vast terrace was leveled on the Vatican Hill and the basilica, when built [starting in the late 320s], was 391 feet (119m) long and 210 feet (64m) wide. [The altar was] at the western end the building.[22]

Along with the Christian faith itself, Saint Peter's and several other Christian churches survived western Rome's collapse in the late 400s and early 500s. In these same years eastern Rome, centered at Constantinople, on the Black Sea's southern rim, survived and over time mutated into the Byzantine Empire. Its largest and finest Christian church, Hagia Sophia, erected in the mid-300s, also employed the basic basilica form.

However, the building's designers also added some distinct additions, including an enormous dome hovering directly above the nave. That dome, which was later rebuilt twice, is 102 feet (31m) in diameter. The architectural device of a rectangular-shaped hall surmounted by a great dome became a key feature of Byzantine churches. Representing the emerging Eastern Orthodox branch of Christianity, these were built across Greece and other sectors of eastern Europe in the early medieval centuries.

Meanwhile, the separate western and northern European cultural sphere, where the faith's original Roman Catholic branch prevailed, was still reeling from the barbarian invasions. So no large-scale program of church building occurred for more than two centuries after western Rome's demise. A moderate burst of such construction did take place under Charlemagne (reigned 768–814), a Frankish (early French) ruler who carved out a realm that included large portions of Europe. Attempting to revive the old Roman Empire, Charlemagne had himself crowned Roman Emperor on Christmas Day in 800. Among his personal attributes was strong religious devotion, which inspired him to build churches, including the splendid Palatine Chapel in his capital, Aachen, Germany. His biographer, the Frankish scholar Einhard, wrote:

> The Christian religion, in which he had been brought up from infancy, was held by [Charlemagne] as most sacred, and he worshiped in it with the greatest piety. For this reason he built at Aachen a most beautiful church, which he enriched with gold and silver, and candlesticks, and also with lattices and doors of solid brass. When columns and marbles for the building could not be obtained from elsewhere, he had them brought from Rome. . . . He provided for the church an abundance of sacred vessels of gold and silver.[23]

The chapel at Aachen, completed in 805, has various architectural features that were clearly derived from ancient Roman buildings. They include arches, vaults, Corinthian pillars, and a high ceiling that creates a feeling of immense interior space. The oval-shaped (technically octagonal-shaped) nave was copied from a late Roman basilica in Ravenna, in northern Italy.

On the chapel's exterior near the front entrance looms a non-Roman touch introduced by Charlemagne's immediate French predecessors—a westwork, essentially a stone tower built for security purposes. Containing a gallery facing inward and overlooking the chapel's nave, it "gave the emperor an unobstructed view of the ceremonies at the high altar," one expert

Built in the fifth century B.C., the magnificent Hagia Sophia in Istanbul set the standard for basilica-style architecture in the early medieval period. Shown here are the nave, or central hall, and the imposing central dome.

explains, "and at the same time ensured his privacy and safety."[24] Thereafter, westworks became regular features of churches in France, Germany, and some other parts of medieval Europe.

Romanesque Churches

A second and considerably larger explosion of European church building began shortly after the turn of the first Christian millennium in 1000. "Especially in Italy and France," Raul Glaber, a French monk of the time, wrote, there was a widespread "rebuilding of church basilicas." He added, "It was as if the whole Earth, having cast off the old by shaking itself, were clothing itself everywhere in the white robe of the church . . .

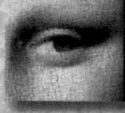

THE MASTER BUILDERS

In the early to mid-medieval centuries, the men who were in charge of erecting churches and other large buildings were called master builders, or master masons. Such a person was a kind of jack-of-all-trades, who typically began by mastering one craft and then became adept in others over time. Such builders commonly traveled long distances in search of work (as accurately depicted in Ken Follett's popular historical novel *The Pillars of the Earth*, in which the lead character is a medieval master builder). Having completed a church or other building to the satisfaction of those who had hired him, the builder, along with his family (if any) and assistants (including masons or carpenters of lesser experience and status), moved on to the next job. Such a job could last from a few weeks or months to several years, depending on the size and complexity of the project. While at a given worksite, the builder and his assistants lived either in some small rooms above or adjacent to their workshop, or in the case of larger projects, in bigger, more comfortable lodgings provided by their employer.

and likewise the monasteries of the various saints, as well as the lesser places of prayer [i.e., local chapels] in the towns."[25]

The new and mighty burst of religious building marked the start of what art historians call the Romanesque period of architecture and other arts. *Romanesque* means "in the Roman manner," so it is not surprising that the new structures bore a strong resemblance to older Roman buildings, in particular basilicas.

Like earlier medieval Christian churches, including those erected by Charlemagne, the ones that appeared in the Romanesque period used large, rectangular blocks of stone and rounded arches, both trademarks of Roman construction. One principal difference between the newer and older versions was the composition and structure of the roofs. Those of earlier Christian churches had been made of wooden timbers. In contrast, the roofs of many Romanesque churches were composed of masonry (stone) vaults, frequently supported by wide supporting arches called ribs.

Another difference between the earlier churches and those of the formal Romanesque period was the size and degree of ornamentation in the interiors of the newer ones. Their naves and apses were decorated with numerous sculptures and wall paintings, along with expensive, finely made chandeliers and magnificent altars surmounted by hand-carved holy objects inlaid with gems and large-scale crucifixes made of gold. An excellent example is the Saint-Sernin Basilica in Toulouse, France, described here by an authority on Western sacred art:

> There are 268 [decorated column] capitals throughout the interior . . . most [of them] carved with foliage decorations but some [with] narrative scenes, such as *Daniel in the Lions' Den.* . . . The north transept contains medieval frescoes that were only discovered in the 1970s, when the 19th-century plaster was removed from the walls. Dating from around 1180, these include a *Resurrection of Christ* in five scenes [and] an angel seated on clouds. . . . The high altar itself, however, is a rare and important Romanesque survival. It is inscribed with the date of its consecration, May 24, 1096,

and the signature of its maker, Bernardus Gilduinus. The marble altar is finely carved around the edges with reliefs of angels, birds, foliage and other motifs.[26]

With so many large-scale, highly decorated religious structures going up across Europe, there was an increasing need for talented and reliable sculptors, painters, goldsmiths, and other artists to work on them. Most in demand, however, were architects. It is important to emphasize that these individuals were not exactly equivalent to their modern counterparts. They did not create precise blueprints, for instance. Instead they came up with basic designs, made sketches of them, and stood by onsite to make sure that all the construction steps and decorative

The interior of the Saint-Sernin Basilica in Toulouse, France, is an excellent example of design from the Romanesque period. Seen here are some of the 268 decorated columns within its walls.

details were executed correctly. The most common term for such a person was *master builder*, or *master mason*. A master builder was both "a structural engineer and building contractor," Nicola Coldstream explains. "He organized supplies of stone, sub-contracted his team of masons, [and] sometimes administered the finances. He became a master not through academic study, but by training within the building industry."[27]

Gothic's Soaring Spires

European master builders, especially those in France, were constantly trying out new materials, techniques, and stylistic variations. This experimentation led to the invention of a new style of architecture in the mid- to late twelfth century—Gothic. The older churches, in the Romanesque style, had small windows that let in limited amounts of light. The keys to the newer Gothic style were structural elements that allowed builders to add a number of large stained glass windows. These flooded the vast interiors of these buildings with light. In a way, some experts have noted, the block-like solidity of Romanesque walls were replaced by what were, for all intents and purposes, translucent walls.

Moreover, in their zeal to glorify God, Gothic builders strove for huge size and height in their structures, as well as ornate, at times visually overwhelming, detail. Summarizing the historical place and spirit of the new style, Stokstad says:

> By the mid-twelfth century in western Europe, a combination of technological skill, material resources, and intellectual and spiritual motivation created an art and architecture that expressed the dedicated religious belief of the Christian community. . . . Bishops, abbots, and civic leaders vied to build and decorate the largest, richest churches. Just as residents of twentieth-century American cities raced to erect higher and higher skyscrapers, so too the bishops of medieval western Europe competed in the building of cathedrals and parish churches with tall naves and soaring towers.[28]

The Cathedral of Notre Dame features the flying buttresses that were so integral to Gothic design.

One of the most important structural elements that allowed builders to achieve such towering sacred spires was the flying buttress. Gothic cathedrals, such as the one completed in Chartres, France, in the 1220s, had such enormous upper sections that their weight pressed both downward and outward with tremendous force. The outward-thrusting forces had to be contained in order to keep the building from collapsing. To accomplish this formidable task, master builders developed the flying buttress. Simply stated, it consists of a partial section of a stone arch installed on a building's exterior flank in such a

Unfortunately for modern historians and other scholars, the names and personal information of extremely few medieval masons, carpenters, and other builders have survived. Among those few are two Frenchmen, William of Sens, who lived and worked in the 1100s, and Villard de Honnecourt, from the century that followed. The particulars of William of Sens's life are largely a mystery. But evidence suggests that he renovated sections of Canterbury Cathedral, in southern England, after the structure was ravaged by fire. As for Honnecourt, his life is also mostly a blank slate. However, various facts about his work and his personal approach to architecture are known because he left behind a journal known as the *Album*. "From Villard's *Album*," scholar Marjorie Rowling writes, "we can deduce something of his knowledge of the technique of architecture." The work contains Honnecourt's excellent drawings of the

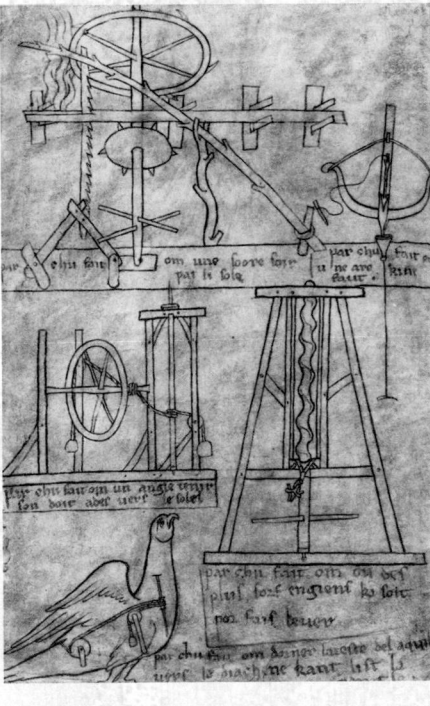

Laon and Reims Cathedrals, showing what part of them looked like in his day. He also included sketches of lifting devices and other simple machines of the era. Honnecourt's tombstone, in Reims Cathedral, has an image of him holding a measuring rod, one of the symbols of proud medieval builders.

Marjorie Rowling. *Life in Medieval Times*. New York: Berkeley, 1987, p. 167.

The journal known as The Album of Villard de Honnecourt *contains illustrations of the cathedrals of Laon and Reims, as well as many drawings of the machinery used in their construction.*

way that it leans inward against the vertical supports. This inward force counterbalances the outward thrust of the structure's upper sections.

Flying buttresses and other elements of Gothic architecture, Marjorie Rowling points out, allowed for constructing buildings so immense that many Europeans viewed them as magical and enchanting. "To men previously accustomed to the solid, down-to-earth qualities of Romanesque buildings," she says, "the graceful pillars and arches, the flying buttresses . . . the beauty of rose windows with their jewel-like stained glass, and of slender pinnacles soaring towards the sky must have appeared miraculous even to their makers."[29]

The first European cathedral erected fully in the Gothic style was the Basilica of Saint-Denis in Paris, completed in 1144. Its Gothic spires, stained glass windows, and other architectural elements were conceived to glorify God, a goal revealed in these surviving remarks by Abbot Suger, the priest who designed the structure:

> The nave is supported by 12 columns, corresponding to the twelve apostles, with just as many in the aisles, corresponding to the 12 prophets. . . . [On entering] you are no longer guests and strangers, but fellow-citizens with the saints and members of God's house, which is built upon the foundation of the apostles and the prophets, with Jesus as the cornerstone unifying both walls, [and which] grows to become a holy temple in the Lord.[30]

Brunelleschi's Dome

Some of these "holy temples," including the one in Chartres and the famous Notre Dame Cathedral in Paris, were so immense and splendid that many fourteenth-century Europeans thought they would never be surpassed. This assumption proved wrong, however. As happened with Europe's secular buildings, its churches and other religious structures passed from the Gothic phase to the Renaissance period in the early

Filippo Brunelleschi's huge dome for the Basilica of Saint Mary in Florence, Italy, was based on the design of the Pantheon in Rome.

1400s. In the process, those churches underwent a new flowering of artistic forms and ideas.

These ideas, which became characteristic of religious architecture in the Renaissance, were the same ones that inspired the designs for secular architecture in that era. They included the creation of large interior spaces, the efficient use of perspective and proper proportions, and a fascination for classical styles and concepts. Among the latter were depictions of events and scenes from Greek and Roman myths; columns utilizing the three Greco-Roman orders (especially the lavish Corinthian); and increased emphasis on the nude human body, which had been common in classical art. Another prevalent feature of Renaissance art was a distinct trend toward naturalism, or the attempt to make people, animals, and objects look as realistic as possible.

Three of these prevailing elements of Renaissance art—the creation of interior space, proper use of proportion, and love of classical building styles and elements—came together in one of the first great religious structures of the period. It was the dome for the Basilica of Saint Mary of the Flowers in Florence. By the late 1300s that northern Italian city-state had blossomed into a politically and culturally influential state. Neighboring Italian states competed with and tried to surpass it on a regular basis. So its rulers sought to retain their power and prestige in part by outdoing all others in the creation of magnificent public buildings.

These buildings included churches, of which Saint Mary's was one of the leading examples. After many years of on-and-off construction, in 1418 it was complete except for its dome, which a succession of designers had intended to be the largest built since ancient Roman times—137 feet (42m) wide at its base. But none of these builders was exactly sure how to erect a dome that immense. So the city fathers decided to run a contest to find an architect with a workable design.

The winner was Filippo Brunelleschi, a Florentine by birth who had spent several years in Rome. There he had surveyed the surviving remnants of that city's ancient buildings, which had impressed him so much that he had chosen to pursue a career designing similar large-scale structures. On hearing about the contest in his native city, he closely examined the enormous masonry dome of Rome's ancient Pantheon, which was still in nearly pristine condition. Brunelleschi concluded that the Pantheon's dome, then the largest in Europe, had survived for so many centuries primarily because the builders had cleverly reduced its overall weight. They had accomplished this by coffering, or partly hollowing out, the stones comprising the huge hemisphere.

Brunelleschi decided that his new masonry dome for Saint Mary's would also be coffered. In addition, he planned a novel design in which one relatively thin dome encased another thin one. Numerous iron and stone ribs joined the inner dome to the outer one, leaving mainly empty space between. The brilliance of this concept was that the two domes together weighed less than a single thicker one. Also, most of the existing weight rested on the ribs, which transferred it downward through the vertical supports in the church's walls.

The Culmination

Brunelleschi's dome was finished in 1436. He also worked on other churches and chapels in Florence, among them the Basilica of Saint Lawrence, also known as San Lorenzo. His use of mathematical proportion in that stunning structure was widely imitated by architects across Europe for the remainder of the Renaissance and well beyond. In some cases later architects made important additions to churches that he and other early Renaissance designers had created. For example, two domes, one large and one small, were added to San Lorenzo more than a century after Brunelleschi's death.

In fact, the dome became the chief architectural symbol of Renaissance churches, much as the towering spire had been the visual trademark of Gothic cathedrals. A dome rivaling Brunelleschi's is a key component of Rome's Saint Peter's Basilica, part of the Vatican, the official home of the Roman Catholic Church. Architecturally speaking, Saint Peter's is a

THE GOTHIC LOVER

Of the prominent figures who lived in the early years of the Gothic period of medieval art, one of the most important was churchman, historian, and avid promoter of Gothic architecture Abbot Suger. Born somewhere in France in about 1011, as a child he was educated at the Basilica of Saint-Denis, not far north of Paris. In young manhood, he met the future king of France, Louis VI, and the two became friends. In 1118 Louis, now on the throne, made Suger his ambassador to the pope in Italy, where the young clergyman spent the next four years. Returning home in 1122 or 1123, Suger became the abbot of Saint-Denis, then a Romanesque building. Entranced by the idea of installing windows in churches that would let in large amounts of light, he became a big supporter of Gothic building. It appears that Suger hired one or more master builders to begin Saint-Denis's transformation into a Gothic structure. He described the renovation in writings that have survived.

striking marriage of a great dome and a basilica with huge inner space. The original basilica on the spot, erected in the 300s, was torn down in 1506, and a new one was built in stages over the course of the next century.

Michelangelo designed the core of the basilica. His floor plan was in the form of a Greek, or square-shaped, cross. Later, architect Carlo Maderno extended one end of the basilica to make it form the Latin, or rectangular-shaped, cross. The design of the enormous dome was also Michelangelo's, although architect Giacomo della Porta and engineer Domenico Fontana later tweaked it slightly. (The dome subsequently inspired those of Saint Paul's Cathedral in London and the U.S. Capitol in Washington, D.C.) Finally, architect Gian Lorenzo Bernini added the great square with its colossal colonnades (rows of columns) in front of the basilica. The magnificent finished product—combining basilica, dome, and square—remains the culmination of Renaissance architecture and a true triumph of human artistic achievement.

3

Sculpture: Romanesque to Renaissance

Medieval European sculpture followed a path similar to that of monumental architecture. Both were major categories of artistic endeavor in the ancient Greco-Roman world, and both fell into near obscurity in the immediate aftermath of western Rome's fall. Also like large-scale architecture, major sculptural efforts slowly regained momentum and importance over time, reaching their height during the Renaissance.

Early Medieval Sculptures

Before about A.D. 1000, most examples of sculpture in medieval Europe were small—usually from a few inches up to 1 foot (30cm) or so in length. Larger pieces included a few finely carved thrones and caskets for the nobility. Moreover, early medieval sculptures were crafted from a limited number of materials, mainly wood, bone, and ivory, the latter being especially popular. Stone carvings were rare, and virtually no large-scale stone sculptures, including life-size statues of people and animals, were created in medieval Europe before the eleventh century.

More typical early medieval carvings included wooden or ivory crucifixes used in worship; small figurines, frequently of Jesus's apostles or various saints; ornate covers for church books; altarpieces (decorative works placed on church altars);

Among the early medieval sculptures were wooden carvings like this one, expertly executed in low relief.

and decorations for reliquaries, containers for bones, pieces of clothing, and other objects connected to saints or other religious figures and therefore viewed as holy. The book covers and altarpieces often took the form of diptychs. A diptych (DIP-tik) consists of two carved panels connected by a hinge, so that the faces fold together. (There is also the triptych, with three hinged panels, the tetraptych, with four, and so forth, although the diptych is the most common.) The figures and scenes carved on such panels were generally in low relief, or only slightly raised from the flat background.

One of the finest surviving examples of a sculpted medieval book cover is the front of the so-called Lorsch Gospels, a Bible made in southern Germany in about 810, during the height of Charlemagne's reign. Divided into five sections, the ivory work portrays several biblical characters in tremendous detail. In the top sections, angels hold a carved cameo of the adult Jesus, while in the center, Mary cradles the baby Jesus, flanked on the left by John the Baptist and on the right by the prophet Zacharias. The bottom section shows a nativity, or birth story, depicting the manger Jesus was said to be born in, sheep and other animals, an angel, and Roman buildings in the background.

Among the larger surviving early medieval carvings is a beautifully made throne of wood and ivory from sixth-century Ravenna. It was made for that city's archbishop, Maximianus, who served from 546 to 556. Bryn Mawr College scholar James Snyder says:

> The body of the throne is completely covered with large ivory plaques fitted to the structural [framework] of wood. The legs and posts are lined with ivory strips with intricate [carvings] peopled by tiny animals and birds. Across the front are five vertical panels portraying John the Baptist, flanked by standing figures of the four [writers of the Gospels]. Their stances are subtly varied, and ripples of movement are created by the shifting of their weight, the raising of arms, [and] the large whorls of drapery spinning across their torsos. . . . The sides of the throne are bedecked with rectangular

panels . . . that relate the story of Joseph in Egypt. In these narratives a surprisingly rich, flickering texture predominates, too.[31]

Romanesque Carvings

The various early medieval carvings, though at times very skillfully executed and beautiful, provided a mere foretaste of the full potential of sculpture in the era. The eventual return of larger-scale and more ambitious sculptures, particularly stone ones, was a consequence of the great outburst of church building that began shortly after the year 1000 and set the Romanesque period of art in motion. The new, highly motivated church builders wanted these buildings to glorify God as much as possible. So in addition to designing imposing architectural exteriors and interiors, they decorated them, especially the interiors, with bigger, more impressive sculptures than had existed in Europe since Rome's last century.

Indeed, beginning in the Romanesque period and continuing for centuries to come, there was a close and vital working relationship between sculpture and architecture. Each helped to increase the grandeur and appeal of the other, in part because the sculptures often seemed to grow organically out of the architecture. Conversely, the architecture appeared to frame and showcase the carvings perfectly.

This was particularly evident in Romanesque portal sculptures, those located above and around the main entrances of churches. The largest portal space was the tympanum, the hemispherical area directly above the doors. A magnificent example of stone relief within that space is the tympanum of the Cathedral of Saint Lazare, in Autun, France, built between 1120 and 1135. According to one prominent art historian, Jesus

> presides in judgment over the cowering, naked figures of the resurrected humans at his feet. The damned writhe in torment at [his] left . . . while the saved, praying, reach toward heaven on Christ's right. [Below], angels help other souls to rise from their graves, while

An outstanding
example of medieval
stone carving, this
relief of *The Last
Judgment* appears on
the tympanum of the
Cathedral of Saint
Lazare in Autun,
France.

a pair of giant, pincer-like hands descends at the far
right to snatch one of the damned into hell. Above
these hands . . . the archangel Michael oversees the
weighing of souls on the scales of good and evil.[32]

In the Autun Cathedral and many other Romanesque
churches, relief sculptures also adorned the archivolts (the
moldings following the curve of the arch above the tympanum);
the trumeau (the supporting post in the center, between the
front doors); and the column capitals, often substituting for

the leaves in Corinthian pillars. In general, these reliefs were a good deal higher, or more raised, than those in earlier medieval carvings. In fact, some figures look as if they are barely attached to the flat background.

An excellent example exists on the capital of a stone column in the Autun Cathedral's nave. It consists of a beautiful carving showing an angel awakening the Magi, the three wise men (in medieval times seen as kings) often depicted visiting Jesus shortly after his birth in the manger. The angel points to the star of Bethlehem, carved at the top of the pillar, completing a scene that in Marilyn Stokstad's words "communicates the key elements of the story with wonderful economy and clarity."[33] The sculptor, thought by many scholars to be a French artist, Gislebertus, carved the figures so that they look almost fully three-dimensional. But their backs are in fact attached to the capital. (Other experts think Gislebertus was more likely the churchman or wealthy patron who hired the sculptor and other artisans.)

Gothic Detail and Drama

During the Gothic period of art that followed on the heels of the Romanesque, sculptors continued to decorate churches and other buildings with finely carved reliefs on tympanums, doors, columns, and walls, along with altarpieces, reliquaries, and other decorations. The newer carvings were similar in many ways to those that had come before. However, there were also some significant differences. First, Gothic sculptures tended to be more naturalistic, as well as more detailed, so much so that the viewer often must linger a while in order not to miss some of the tiny, intricate features.

Illustrative of such detail are the elaborate sculpted pulpits created by the Pisano family of gifted sculptors in northern Italy. A single section of Nicola Pisano's pulpit for Siena Cathedral, completed in 1268, displays Jesus's nativity scene in high relief with some twenty human figures, plus several animals and the upper story of a large house. The details, notably in the people's faces and the folds of their robes and other clothing, are nothing short of breathtaking.

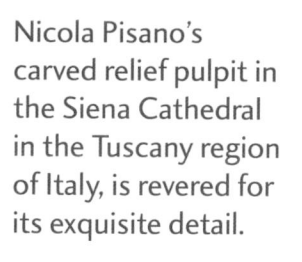

Nicola Pisano's carved relief pulpit in the Siena Cathedral in the Tuscany region of Italy, is revered for its exquisite detail.

A second difference between Romanesque and Gothic sculpture is that the latter was frequently carved in higher relief. Indeed, some of the human figures in Gothic carvings are nearly completely freestanding statues, with only a hip, an elbow, or the drape of a robe still connecting them to a wall, door frame, or column. An outstanding example survives in the remnants of the mostly destroyed Charterhouse of Champmol, near Dijon, France. A family tomb established in 1383 by nobleman Philip the Bold, it contained the *Well of Moses*, a splendid sculpted monument for the tomb of Philip's son, John the Fearless. The main theme of the work, carved by the great Dutch sculptor

Claus Sluter, was Jesus's crucifixion. Large parts of the scene have been lost, but much of the base has survived almost completely intact and remains in view in the hospital later built on the site. The hexagonal base contains six life-size figures of biblical prophets—Moses, David, Jeremiah, Zachariah, Daniel, and Isaiah. Each is attached to the base, yet appears to be trying to pull free and walk away. These figures demonstrate Sluter's "extraordinary observation of detail, in which he was far ahead of his time,"[34] scholar Uwe Geese writes.

Sluter's grouping of sculpted figures for the front portal of the Charterhouse demonstrates a third characteristic of Gothic sculpture. This is its extraordinary degree of order, organization, and overall dramatic effect. The central figure in the grouping, positioned in the trumeau, is Mary, who is holding the baby Jesus. In stark contrast to the more static poses of Romanesque figures, she rests her weight on her left leg and thrusts her right leg outward, her body and robes contributing to her tilted, theatrical pose. Four other figures, two in each door jamb, turn inward toward her in their own dynamic poses, overall creating a highly dramatic effect.

Ghiberti's Doors

By the early 1400s this increasing sense of organization, energy, and drama, along with a rising degree of realism, led European sculptors into the emerging Renaissance. As was the case with architecture and most other arts in the period, Italy led the way in sculpture, with Florence once again in the forefront. Indeed, in the same years that Brunelleschi was designing and raising his famous dome, in that same city sculptor Lorenzo Ghiberti (gee-BEAR-tee, born 1378) was making his mark.

In fact, Ghiberti and Brunelleschi were both among a group of young artists who competed for a choice commission in 1401. The clergy of the Florence Baptistery, an older religious structure built in the Romanesque style, wanted to install a set of bronze doors with panels containing sculpted scenes from the Bible. Although the judges gave Brunelleschi high ratings, awarding him second place, Ghiberti won the competition.

Ghiberti set up a large workshop and hired several assistants, some of whom later became famous sculptors. Together they completed the doors, which depicted twenty-eight scenes from the New Testament. Afterward, in 1425, Ghiberti received a second commission from the baptistery, this time for gilded bronze doors showing scenes from the Old Testament. The sculpted figures made for this second set of doors were so detailed, lifelike, and dramatic that the great Michelangelo was awestruck. He nicknamed them *The Gates of Paradise*, a name that stuck. (Michelangelo later borrowed the pose Ghiberti gave the Old Testament's first man, Adam, and used it for his own Adam in the famous Sistine Chapel paintings.) Ghiberti's scenes for these doors later came to be seen as the first great sculptural work of the Renaissance. Art critic John Haber remarks, "*The Gates of Paradise* consist of ten panels—one column of five panels to each side of the seventeen-foot [5.1m]-high double doors . From the story of Adam and Eve at the top left to Solomon at the bottom right, each panel represents a succession of events. Often the same characters appear two or three times. The scheme allows Ghiberti to make each panel an entire narrative."[35]

Donatello and Michelangelo

Among the young Florentine sculptors who trained with Ghiberti was Donatello (born Donato di Niccolo di Betto Bardi in 1386). Donatello started out working on Gothic churches (which were still being built) and sometimes made his living as a goldsmith. He excelled at all forms of sculpture and worked equally well in materials ranging from wood and stone to bronze and gold. Also, he was constantly experimenting with new ideas and techniques, breaking new ground with almost every major work. It is no wonder that he became the most influential sculptor of the early Renaissance, greatly inspiring Michelangelo among many others.

Like other Renaissance artists, Donatello eagerly revived classical styles and concepts while adapting them to his own needs. Large freestanding statues were key forms in classical

GHIBERTI'S SATISFIED SMILE

In anticipation of a 2008 U.S. exhibition of panels from Lorenzo Ghiberti's renowned bronze doors for the Florence Baptistery, American journalist Arthur Lubow wrote in part:

Ghiberti's doors were instantly recognized as a masterpiece. As one commentator declared in the 1470s, "nothing like them had been done before on the globe and through them the name of man shines everywhere.". . . The third panel, "Jacob and Esau," is Ghiberti's most masterful. "It best demonstrates his genius," says Syracuse University professor Gary Radke, the curator of the exhibition, because "it shows so many aspects of Renaissance art." The receding tiles of the floor illustrate the [Renaissance] innovation of scientific perspective, and the arches and pilasters are inspired by Roman architecture. . . . Ghiberti also played here with sculptural illusion by extending some of his figures almost off the panel, while depicting others in low relief. The artist apparently shared posterity's high regard for this achievement. "Ghiberti put his own self-portrait and his signature right under it," Radke notes. The self-portrait bust shows a bald man of about 60, with a shrewd gaze and a thin, broad mouth that seems to be smiling with self-satisfaction.

Arthur Lubow. "The Gates of Paradise." Smithsonian.com. www.smithsonianmag.com/arts-culture/gates ofparadise-200711.html.

Depicting the biblical tale of Jacob and Esau, this panel of Ghiberti's doors incorporates many aspects of Renaissance art and has been called a work of genius.

Donatello excelled in all forms of sculpture and used wood, stone, bronze, and gold in his work. Shown here is his *Madonna with Child*, sculpted in wood and painted.

antiquity, so he daringly carved the first life-size freestanding stone statue made in Europe since Rome's demise. Depicting the Christian saint Mark, it was created for a niche of Florence's Church of Orsanmichele. He also sculpted a freestanding statue of Saint George for the same church (with an elegant sculpted relief of Saint George slaying a dragon on the front of the statue's base). Another important work by Donatello was a magnificent rendering of the biblical character David (of uncertain date, but likely completed in the mid-1440s). It was the first freestanding life-size nude statue created since ancient times. About this masterpiece, Elke Linda Buchholz says:

> Wearing a hat and boots, the biblical shepherd boy sets his foot carelessly on the decapitated head of the defeated Goliath. Donatello understood the human body as a living organism, whose parts form a harmonious whole. Surprising is the tender, almost feminine form of the body. It represents ideal beauty but is realistically

rendered down to the smallest detail. The harmony of the proportions and the steady posture show David's inner peace. . . . [Donatello's] free-standing statues exhibit a dignity and realism that had not been seen since antiquity. His works embodied the new ideal man of the Renaissance and showed people as self-determined individuals, powerful and intellectually alive.[36]

Michelangelo was not only strongly influenced by Donatello, but also one of the few later sculptors who can be said to have surpassed him. The greatest sculptor of the Renaissance (and in the opinion of some experts of all time), Michelangelo saw the human body as the most beautiful form in existence. Moreover, he believed that such a body lay latent in both a sculptor's mind and the raw stone block he approached to carve. Therefore, the sculptor's main task was to free that body from its stone prison. Michelangelo reportedly said, "In hard and craggy stone, the mere removal of the surface gives being to a figure, which ever grows the more the stone is hewn away."[37]

This singular psychological approach to his art, coupled with his phenomenal talent, allowed Michelangelo to create large-scale sculptures of unprecedented beauty and majesty. One of these pieces, the *Pietà*, commissioned in 1497, portrays Mary holding her son Jesus's body shortly after his crucifixion. The Renaissance biographer Vasari expressed the general consensus of people in that era when he remarked that it was hard to believe that a mere human could have carved it.

Contemporary views (along with modern ones) of a much larger sculpture created by Michelangelo were just as flattering. His *David*, begun in 1501 and standing 17 feet (5.2m) high, was the largest freestanding statue carved in Europe in more than one thousand years. Commissioned by a group of well-to-do wool merchants, when completed in 1504 the statue was placed in front of Florence's town hall, where it stood for more than three centuries. (In 1873 it was moved to a Florentine art academy and a replica was put in its place at the town hall.)

Michelangelo began work on his *David* statue in 1501. The sculpture is 17 feet high and is perhaps the most famous statue in the world. Many think Michelangelo is the greatest sculptor of all time.

A SYSTEM OF MENTORSHIP

One reason that the European Renaissance produced large numbers of skilled sculptors and other artists, especially in Italy, was that most of these talented individuals emerged from a well-entrenched system of apprenticeship and mentorship. In it young, inexperienced artists trained with older, experienced ones and in some cases became their assistants or close collaborators for years afterward. When the younger artists became masters, they, too, took on and trained younger people who showed promise. A case in point was the succession of fine artists that began with Lorenzo Ghiberti in the early 1400s. That expert sculptor taught and employed Donato di Niccolo di Betto Bardi, better known as Donatello, widely seen as the first great sculptor of the Renaissance. In his turn, Donatello taught Bartolomeo Bellano (or Vellano, born circa 1437), the son of a goldsmith who later built his own major reputation and became known for a sculpture called *Europa and the Bull* (depicting a famous incident from Greek mythology). Bellano then mentored Andrea Riccio (born circa 1470). As a successful sculptor in his own right, Riccio became known for creating small-scale bronze objects, such as door knockers, which he executed in tremendous, ornate detail. His works eventually became widely popular with art collectors across Europe.

Michelangelo's statues ensured Florence's continued domination of the art of sculpture in the Renaissance. Many sculptors across Europe turned out striking works during the period. But none surpassed those of the Florentines. Another artist of that city, Benvenuto Cellini (born 1500), himself a gifted sculptor, is reported to have said proudly, "Donatello and the great Michelangelo [are] men that in the glory of their works have beaten the ancients."[38]

4

Evolving Painting Forms and Techniques

L arge, colorful paintings were a staple of Greco-Roman art. Many were wall or ceiling murals, while others were portable paintings, those done on wood panels, parchment, or other materials that could be carried from place to place. (A majority of modern paintings, done on canvas, are portable.) After the collapse of the western Roman Empire in the fifth and sixth centuries, the production of traditional paintings, both portable and nonportable, temporarily ceased in western Europe.

In the eastern Mediterranean region, meanwhile, where Rome's eastern provinces survived and mutated into the Byzantine Empire, traditional painting forms survived, too. However, the themes and look of Byzantine paintings were very different from those that had come before. In the fourth and fifth centuries, Christianity had risen to power in Rome and was particularly strong and influential in Constantinople, which became the Byzantine capital. Before the Christian revolution, murals and other paintings had typically portrayed gods, heroes, and monsters from classical mythology. With Christianity's rise, these were swiftly replaced by images of Jesus; his mother, Mary; and the apostles and saints.

Byzantine religious paintings came to be called icons. They had a standardized look, with very little variation in subjects, poses, and overall style. Also, though attractive in their own right, they had a formal, flat look with little or no use of perspective and shading. In addition, because of the power of Byzantine religious tradition, originality and experimentation among artists was frowned on. As Roy Bolten says, "The Eastern Church entered into a period of artistic limbo, producing icons that [were] copies or variations of existing paintings. . . . [So] the art of a vast region of eastern Europe and the [Middle] East stood still for 1,000 years."[39]

In western Europe when artists began painting again, their work was, at first, very small scale. It consisted of carefully crafted illustrations for religious books, most often versions of the Bible. These came to be known as illuminated manuscripts.

Early Byzantine artists often showed the influence of Christianity in their religious icons, creating images of Jesus, the Virgin Mary, and the apostles and saints.

Eventually more familiar kinds of painting, including large-scale murals, returned in Europe. Initially these works were highly influenced by and largely mimicked Byzantine styles and subjects. But unlike the situation in the East, the western versions underwent a rapid evolution that culminated in some of history's most magnificent paintings during the Renaissance.

Illuminated Manuscripts

The first steps in this evolution were illuminated manuscripts of Ireland and Anglo-Saxon England between about 650 and 800. They began with the decoration of a few letters, usually the first letter in the first word of a biblical book or chapter.

The title page of the Gospel of John from the Lindisfarne Gospels is pictured here.

MEDIEVAL PAINTS

When preparing to begin work, medieval panel painters first created a suitable surface by coating the wooden panels with strips of linen soaked in gesso (a mixture of plaster and glue). Then they applied a kind of paint often called tempera. It was made by mixing a powdered pigment with egg yolk, a small amount of water, and sometimes a bit of glue. Usually the painter's apprentice (or apprentices) made the paints, mixing them in small wooden bowls or dishes made from seashells. This approach changed significantly in the 1400s with the introduction of oil-based paints. Dutch artists had experimented with oil paints for several generations. Finally, Dutchman Jan van Eyck (born circa 1395) perfected them, showing that they were superior to tempera for creating elaborate detail. Van Eyck popularized oil paints in northern Europe, while Venetian painter Giovanni Bellini (born circa 1431), who admired Van Eyck's work, introduced them to Italy. Thereafter, a majority of painters worked in oils.

The illustrator, almost always a monk working in a monastery, made the letter as flowery and colorful as possible. These images quickly expanded into entire painted pages, most often consisting of complex, ornamented designs, plant stems and leaves, and occasional human faces, rather than full human figures and landscapes. One of the finest surviving examples is the Lindisfarne Gospels, produced by Scottish monks in about 700. "The beginning of the Gospel of John," art historian Susanne Kaeppele explains, "was embellished with tracery [delicately interlaced lines], rhombuses [diamond shapes], crosses, and other forms. Animal and human heads, plants, and birds, all artistically decorated, add further life to the pages already bursting with an intricate, vibrant display of colors."[40]

Advances in illuminated manuscripts occurred during the Carolingian dynasty (783–900), the line of rulers that produced Charlemagne and his brief but impressive empire in central Europe. Supported by the pious Charlemagne and leading clerics of the day, monks and nuns began producing new handmade Bibles or separate sets of the four Gospels. They labored in workrooms called scriptoriums, most often located in monasteries and convents in Germany and France. The small pictures they made were painted on stretched animal skins, which were then bound together with pages of text to form the books. Most of the artists remained anonymous. But a few did sign their works in a section in the back called a colophon.

The subjects and themes of the illuminations now included human forms, most frequently the evangelists (Matthew, Mark, Luke, and John, the names assigned to the anonymous Gospel writers). The illustrators placed these figures in brightly colored interior rooms or exterior architectural settings in late ancient Roman styles. A beautiful example is "John the Evangelist" from the Lorsch Gospels, dating from about 810. Wearing a Roman outfit, John sits on a comfortable-looking couch framed by a Roman triumphal arch and two Corinthian columns.

After 900, Byzantine styles and themes came to dominate western illuminations. (In part this was because some of the western rulers, notably the emperors Otto II and Otto III, had Byzantine wives.) Biblical scenes became prominent. Also, artists adopted the Byzantine fashion of employing a lot of gold leaf, especially in the nimbuses (halos) surrounding the heads of Jesus, the apostles, and other holy characters. The gold leaf symbolized God's glow, which those nearest to him supposedly basked in.

The Revival of Murals

Some wall murals were created in the last three centuries before the Romanesque period, which for medieval painting began in about 1050. Most of these larger paintings have not survived,

This fragment of a medieval mural in Malles Venosta, Italy, was part of a much larger mural that did not survive.

having been either destroyed or painted over in later ages. Among the few surviving examples are fragments found in Trier, France, and Malles Venosta, in northern Italy. One modern expert estimates that the originals were "monumental compositions of great simplicity, highly figurative [symbolic, in this case religiously so], and deeply expressive, with a flair for bright, warm colors."[41]

Like their predecessors in the classical world, the medieval muralists applied their paints directly to walls, ceilings, or

APPRENTICE PAINTERS

The same sort of apprenticing and mentoring system that existed among successful sculptors during the Renaissance also pertained to painters. Italian painter Cennino Cennini (born circa 1370) left behind this description of the ideal program for apprentice painters:

To begin as a shop-boy studying for one year, to get practice in drawing on the little panel [wooden surface]; next to serve in the shop under some master, to learn how to work at all the branches which pertain to our profession, and to stay and begin the working up of colors; and to learn to boil the sizes [materials used to prepare the surface]; and grind the gessos [sizes made from chalk]; and to get experience in gessoing anconas [the brackets that hold cornices in architecture], and modeling and scraping them; gilding [applying gold leaf] and stamping; [all] for the space of a good six years. Then to get experience in painting, embellishing with mordants [sticky materials used in gilding], making cloths of gold. getting practice in working [painting] on the wall, for six more years drawing all the time, never leaving off [failing to practice], either on holidays or on work days.

Cennino Cennini. *Il Libro dell'Arte*. Excerpted in *Daily Life in Renaissance Italy*, by Charles L. Mee Jr. New York: American Heritage, 1975, p. 88.

other large surfaces using two basic approaches. One was secco, in which the paint was applied to dry plaster. The other was fresco, the art of painting on fresh, or wet plaster. In many cases fresco was considered superior because the paint and plaster dried together, creating a more durable product. In his surviving book about painting, the later Italian painter Cennino Cennini (born 1370) gave a detailed description of the fresco method, saying in part:

> When you want to work on a wall . . . first of all get some lime and some sand, each of them well sifted. [And] wet them up well with water, and . . . let it stand for a day or so, until the heat goes out of it. . . . When you are ready to plaster, first sweep the wall well, and wet it down thoroughly, [and] take your lime mortar . . . a trowel-full at a time, and plaster once or twice, to begin with, to get the plaster flat on the wall. Then . . . take [some] charcoal, and draw [outlines of] the scene or figures which you have to do; and take all your measurements carefully. . . . Then take a small, pointed bristle brush, and a little [paint] as thin as water; and proceed to copy and draw in your figures, shading as you did with washes when you were learning to draw. Then take a bunch of feathers, and sweep the drawing free of the charcoal.[42]

The production of murals expanded significantly during the Romanesque period thanks to the great burst of church building in that era's early years. As Kaeppele says, "Church walls and ceilings were painted extensively, to guide the predominately illiterate churchgoers" through the major biblical stories, as well as to "serve as a form of devotion."[43] Many of the Romanesque murals, particularly in Italy and Germany, displayed strong Byzantine influences.

Gothic Panel Painting

The Romanesque period was also noteworthy for the emergence of panel painting, in which colors were applied to wooden panels of varying thickness. This art form expanded and truly flowered in the Gothic era of painting that began in the late 1100s. Some of the panels were portable, at least before they were installed in a church. But most were very large and heavy, as they were intended as permanent altarpieces or other interior church decorations.

One of the great masterpieces of Gothic panel painting was created by Italian artist Duccio di Buoninsegna (DOO-choh dee bwaw-neen-SEN-yah) and his talented assistants between 1308 and 1311 for the cathedral in Siena. Resting in the center of the church, it was an enormous cluster of panel paintings known as the *Maesta Altarpiece*. The central panel alone, showing the Virgin Mary holding the baby Jesus and surrounded by Christian saints, measured 7 by 13 feet (2m by 4m). Above and below it were numerous smaller panels depicting scenes from Mary's life and Jesus's early years. The people of Siena were so thrilled with the work that they staged a large celebration and a parade to carry it from Duccio's workshop to the cathedral. An eyewitness wrote:

> On the day that it was carried to the [church], the shops were shut, and the bishop conducted a great and devout company of priests and friars in solemn procession, accompanied by . . . all the officers of the [town], and all the people . . . with lighted candles in their hands, took places near the picture, and behind came the women and children with great devotion. And they accompanied the said picture up to the [cathedral], making the procession around the [town square] . . . [with] all the bells ringing joyously, out of reverence for so noble a picture as is this.[44]

Other notable panel paintings were done by two Florentine painters of the era—Cenni di Pepi, better known by his nickname, Cimabue, and his phenomenally talented student, Giotto di Bondone. They include Cimabue's *Virgin and Child Enthroned* (late 1200s) for Florence's Church of Santa Trinita and Giotto's work of the same title (early 1300s) for the Church of the Ognissanti in the same city. Like other Romanesque and Gothic panel paintings, they have a somewhat flat and stylized (purposely exaggerated or unnatural) look. This is reminiscent of Byzantine painting, which continued to influence European artists up to Cimabue's day.

Nevertheless, Cimabue made a number of subtle but important advances that other artists recognized and imitated, including a heightened sense of realism and allowing his subject's

Italian artist Duccio di Buoninsegna created a masterpiece of Gothic panel painting in his *Maesta Altarpiece* in the Siena Cathedral in Italy.

emotions to show. He therefore moved the genre of painting forward. According to Roy Bolton:

> Cimabue took the best of a foreign, static art and developed it into something wonderful. . . . Twice life-size, [his Mary in *Virgin and Child Enthroned*] is a giant looking down at us. Like the flanking angels, she smirks with a palpable sense of superiority. Each figure is painted in new, light pastel shades and the more realistic skin tones that Cimabue had developed, all surrounded by dazzling gold leaf. It was awe-inspiring. Its once immense power as a religious image may have diminished over time, but it is easy to see how these haughty faces from heaven inspired the masses to worship, and the next generation of artists to paint.[45]

Giotto's Bridge

Toward the end of the Gothic period, Giotto matured and produced paintings that in a sense bridged that era with the Renaissance to come. His main accomplishment was to introduce a

Giotto's frescoes, like this panel in the Scrovegni Chapel in Padua, Italy, demonstrate his use of advanced techniques, such as shading, perspective, and background detail.

new sense of naturalism, or realism, that allowed him to surpass other artists, including his mentor, Cimabue. The art critic and chronicler Giorgio Vasari remarked that "Giotto was born in order to give light to painting." Vasari also said that "by the gift of God," Giotto brought the art of painting "to such a form as could be called good. . . . He became so good an imitator of nature that he banished completely that rude [Byzantine] manner and revived the modern and good art of painting."[46]

Several of Giotto's frescoes illustrate his use of realism in rendering human figures. In these paintings he advanced the techniques of shading, perspective, and background detail, giving the figures a degree of thickness and placing them in settings that created the illusion of space, depth, and distance. He also captured human emotions more effectively than any medieval artist before him. These qualities can all be seen in the stunning series of frescoes he completed in 1306 for the interior of the Arena (or Scrovegni) Chapel in Padua, in northern Italy. It consists of about one hundred separate paintings, or scenes, that together form a general narrative related to Jesus, Mary, and other biblical characters. In Marilyn Stokstad's words:

> Events in the life of the Virgin Mary and in the ministry of Jesus are depicted in three registers [rows] that circle the room. . . . Giotto rendered his bulky figures as pure color masses by painting the deepest shadows with the most intense hues and highlighting shapes with lighter shades mixed with white. These sculpturally modeled figures enabled Giotto to convey a sense of depth in both landscape and architectural settings. In [the] paintings, Giotto conveys real human emotions that draw viewers into the scenes.[47]

Giotto's ability to portray human emotions is especially evident in the Arena fresco depicting Mary and others grieving for the crucified Jesus. "The depiction of grief" in the painting, a prominent scholar writes, "is realistic in its varying manifestations. The angels [who look down on the dead Jesus] tear at their hair, scratch their faces, wring their hands in despair, or scream and cry aloud."[48]

The Height of Realism

The trend of increasing realism begun by Cimabue and Giotto accelerated among the early Italian Renaissance artists. Indeed, "the urge to make something that looked absolutely alive seized hold of artists of the Renaissance,"[49] remarks American historian Charles L. Mee. Among those who made important contributions to painting were Masaccio (born 1401), Fra Filippo Lippi (born 1406), Andrea Mantegna (born 1430), and Sandro Botticelli (born 1444). Mantegna was especially influential among painters in other parts of Europe, who began to adopt Italian styles and methods in the mid-to-late 1400s.

The height of the naturalism trend and of Renaissance painting in general came in the early 1500s under a handful of great masters, among them Leonardo da Vinci (born 1452), Michelangelo (born 1475), and Raphael (Raphaello Sanzio, born 1483). Da Vinci was a gifted engineer and inventor as well as a great painter. His most famous paintings are *The Last Supper* (1497) and the *Mona Lisa* (1506). About the innovations the artist achieved in *Mona Lisa*, Bolton says:

> Her body is at an angle, while her head is almost frontal. This was a brand new pose for portraiture. The flesh tones make a strong vertical line, balanced by the horizontal landscape behind. Oddly unequal, the landscape is laid out with aerial perspective. The color and clarity of the distance fades, like reality, the further away you look. This was one of Leonardo's advances. He also built up layers of lightly colored varnish to create the mysterious shadowy depth of her skin. . . . Leonardo's *Mona Lisa* is a real person in a real setting.[50]

Leonardo did not rest on his laurels after completing the *Mona Lisa*. He continued to experiment with new techniques in an effort to make the illusion of reality complete and finally accomplished this goal in his *Last Supper*. "When the painting was fresh," Mee says, "monks entering the room for dinner must have been startled. It would have seemed that Christ and the Apostles were very much alive and having dinner at the refectory in Milan."[51]

LEONARDO'S SKILL IN COMPOSITION

Art critics universally agree that the Virgin and Child with Saint Anne, created between 1501 and 1512, is one of Leonardo da Vinci's finest works. Art historian Elke Linda Buchholz describes the scene it portrays:

St. Anne smiles tenderly upon her daughter, the Virgin Mary, who is sitting upon her lap. She, in turn, bends down with a hint of refrained anxiety toward her son Jesus, who is playing with a lamb. This scene foreshadows his future role as the crucified Lamb of God. Leonardo has composed here a complicated group of people who seem to be in motion, and yet remain closely intertwined. By arranging this composition in the classical form of a pyramid, he lent the picture tranquility [and] compactness. The wide, rocky landscape with mountains disappearing behind the blue fog reflect Leonardo's close observation of nature.

Elke Linda Buchholz et al. *Art: A World History*. New York: Abrams, 2007, p. 145.

Leonardo Da Vinci's Virgin and Child with St. Anne *is considered one of the artist's finest works.*

Incredibly, Michelangelo soon surpassed Leonardo, at least in the grand scope of his works. As a painter, Michelangelo is most famous for the series of paintings he did on the ceiling of the Sistine Chapel, in the Vatican in Rome. They depict the biblical creation of the world, the centerpiece being the moment in which God endows the first human being in the Bible, Adam, with the spark of life. About the narrative of this image, most often called *The Creation of Adam*, one modern expert writes, "God the Father hovers in the air, carried by heavenly beings. He lets the spark of his divine spirit penetrate man. Man, who has been created in God's image, awakens to life. He is no longer a soulless creature, but a creative spirit inspired by the Almighty—a being who strives after divine perfection, as the artists and thinkers of the Renaissance did."[52]

When Michelangelo finished the ceiling, his contemporaries were as awestruck as the people who view it today are. There was and remains a feeling that he elevated the art of realistic, narrative painting to a level that simply cannot be surpassed. Vasari summed it up well when he said, "No man who is a painter need think any more to see new inventions, attitudes, and draperies for the clothing of figures, novel manners of expression, and things painted with greater variety and force, because he gave to this work all the perfection that can be given to any work executed in such a field of art."[53]

Mosaics and Stained Glass: A Dual Role

5

Sculptures and paintings proved to be major means of decorating the interiors of churches during the medieval period. But they were by no means the only artworks included in the construction of religious buildings. Mosaics and stained glass were also widely used, with stained glass windows becoming particularly prominent in the enormous cathedrals that rose in Europe during the Gothic period.

These four arts—stained glass, mosaics, painting, and sculpture—were in the Middle Ages frequently collectively called *Biblia pauperum*, a Latin phrase meaning "poor people's Bible." This referred to the second major function of these artworks in the period. In addition to their decorative function, they were used to educate worshippers about biblical stories and characters. Most of the people who attended medieval churches were poor and illiterate and could not read the Bible themselves. They were unable, for example, to read for themselves the story of the prophet Abraham sacrificing his son Isaac at God's order. However, such a person *could* see the incident graphically portrayed in a painting, or a mosaic, or a panel of stained glass. Thus mosaics and stained glass had a vital dual role in medieval arts and religious society.

Early Christian Mosaics

In its first role as a decorative effect, the medieval mosaic evolved directly from its ancient Roman form. Roman mosaics rose to prominence in Italy in the second and first centuries B.C. and thereafter were used across the Mediterranean world to adorn the floors, walls, and sometimes ceilings of buildings of all types. To create a mosaic, Roman artisans employed thousands of tiny pottery, stone, and/or glass tiles, called tesserae. The standard procedure was to press the tiles into wet concrete and let the concrete dry. Some Roman mosaics depicted decorative geometric or abstract shapes and patterns. Others illustrated people, animals, buildings, and landscapes.

Some of the early fifth century Christian mosaics have survived in the church of Santa Maria Maggiore in Rome.

For centuries, mythical characters and events were particularly popular in Roman mosaics. But there was a radical shift in subject matter after the Christians rose to power in Rome in the fourth century. Under the emperor Constantine I and his successors (all but one of whom were dedicated Christians), numerous Christian churches were built across the empire.

These buildings were liberally decorated with mosaics, which now showed Jesus, Mary, the apostles, and well-known scenes from both the Old and New Testaments.

Some of these elegant artworks have survived in excellent condition. Several adorn the Church of Santa Maria Maggiore, erected in Rome between 432 and 440, a few decades before the last western Roman emperor was deposed in 476. On the nave's walls, high above the floor, can be seen several mosaic scenes depicting biblical stories. One, *The Parting of Lot and Abraham*, shows those two early Hebrew patriarchs parting ways, each with his followers.

Ravenna, which became the western empire's capital in 402, was an important center of early Christian art, and a number of its fine mosaics have survived. Among the more prominent are those in the Mausoleum of Galla Placidia, a small chapel-tomb built in about 425. (Although she was not buried there, the mausoleum was named for this smart, energetic woman who, as regent for her son Valentinian III, ruled the western empire from 425 to 437.) The chapel is packed with beautiful mosaics, most notably in the lunettes, the semicircular wall spaces framed by the ceiling arches. "Floral designs derived from funeral garlands cover the four central arches," a noted art historian says, "and the walls above them are filled with the figures of standing apostles gesturing like orators. Saint Lawrence . . . is represented in the central lunette, [holding] a cross."[54]

Early Medieval Mosaics

After the western empire ceased to exist in the late 400s, existing Christian churches in Italy survived and new ones were built during the early medieval years. So the shift from late Roman or early Christian mosaics to early medieval mosaics was largely uneventful and pretty much seamless. In the East, where the Roman lands began to evolve into the Byzantine realm, mosaics, like painted murals, depicted formulaic, flat, static, but elegant religious scenes. In the West, meanwhile, mosaics, like other aspects of art, continued to be produced mainly in Italy, where Roman traditions were still strong even after western Rome's political demise.

In the 500s, during the first century after that demise, Italian mosaics were strongly influenced by Byzantine models. This was because the eastern emperor Justinian, who ruled in Constantinople from 527 to 565, took Italy back from the Ostrogoths. (They had ruled the region since the last western emperor had vacated the throne in 476). Justinian and his dynamic wife, the empress Theodora, made Ravenna the capital of their Italian province. A large, stunningly decorated new church, San Vitale, dedicated there in 547, survives and contains some of the finest early medieval mosaics. Especially splendid are two that depict the emperor and empress themselves. Yet though these works are beautifully executed, the poses in them, like those in other Byzantine mosaics and paintings, are static, rendering the figures rather lifeless. In Janetta Benton's words:

> The interior of San Vitale . . . is opulent in its ornament, made colorful by mosaics covering all the upper portions. . . . The celebrated mosaics of Justinian and Theodora flank the altar—thus the emperor and empress are portrayed as ever-present worshipers in spite of the fact that neither ever actually visited Ravenna. . . . Although Justinian, Theodora, and possibly other [high officials shown in the mosaics] are specific individuals, everyone is made to look very similar, with large dark eyes, curved eyebrows, long nose, and small mouth—the characteristic Byzantine facial type. . . . In contrast to the relative naturalism seen in early Christian mosaics . . . the Byzantine figures are motionless, their gestures frozen. [The ancient Greco-] Roman concern for realistic [art styles] has now disappeared.[55]

Static or not, these mosaics are impressive for the talent, attention to detail, and sheer perseverance of the artists. Such projects were very time-consuming and laborious to create and required much planning and preparation before the actual artistry began. Indeed, the tiles that made up the faces and bodies of Justinian, Theodora, and their attendants started out as clumps of wet pottery clay. Artisans rolled the clay into a large, flat sheet about half an inch (1.25cm) thick. To cut the clay sheet, two persons grasped either end of a thin but strong thread, pulled it taut, and brought it down onto the sheet. They did this many times, working from top to bottom, then repeated the process working from left to right. Eventually this produced hundreds or thousands of individual tesserae. In the next step, the artisans baked the tiles in a kiln. After removing them and allowing them to cool down, they daubed them with colored glazes and fired them a second time.

While waiting for the tiles to finish baking, the workers prepared the wall or other surface by applying one or more coats of plaster. When the plaster was dry, they used pieces of charcoal to sketch the outlines of the figures and objects in the scene (which had been developed earlier in rough sketches done on parchment). By this time the pottery tesserae were ready

The Church of San Vitale in Ravenna, Italy, dedicated in A.D. 547, contains stunning mosaics of the emperor Justinian and his wife, the empress Theodora, shown here with church bishops.

The interior of the Church of San Vitale has colorful mosaics covering the upper portions of the building.

(perhaps along with pieces of glass, gemstones, or other types of tiles). To apply them, the artisans carefully painted wet, sticky concrete onto the surface and pressed the tiles into the concrete, which dried rock hard.

Later Medieval Mosaics

Large wall and ceiling mosaics continued to be made in Italy after the Byzantines lost control of it to a Germanic tribe, the Lombards, in the late 560s. But such artworks steadily decreased in number, apparently because even after the culturally backward Lombards adopted medieval Christian culture, they favored mosaic floors rather than the wall and ceiling variety. (Having been worn out or replaced over the centuries, nearly all examples of these decorative floors have been lost.)

The situation changed when the Frankish Carolingian dynasty came to power in central Europe in the 700s. Charlemagne soundly defeated the Lombards and incorporated northern Italy into his growing empire. During the mini-renaissance of art he ushered in, mosaics like those created in Ravenna in the 500s once more came into fashion. In the late 700s and early 800s, some beautiful examples were installed in churches in Charlemagne's capital, Aachen, and in Rome. Among the latter were those in the Church of Santi Nereo e Achilleo, including one in the archway leading to the altar, a work that shows the Annunciation. (In Christian tradition, the Annunciation was the announcement the angel Gabriel made to Mary that she would give birth to Jesus.)

Evidence suggests that European expertise in making large mosaics was lost sometime in the 900s. However, in the following two centuries various rulers and churchmen hired Byzantine artisans to travel to Italy and revive the art. Still, although a number of new churches built after 1100 in Italy and elsewhere in Europe featured mosaics, these artworks increasingly came to be seen as too labor-intensive and expensive. So

Charlemagne ushered in a mini-renaissance in the late 700s and early 800s. Shown here, adorned with mosaics, is the interior of the Church of Santi Nereo e Achilleo in Rome.

One reason that many of the splendid mosaics created in early medieval times did not survive is that they were purposely destroyed. Most early medieval mosaics (along with paintings and sculptures) had religious themes and depicted Jesus, Mary, and various apostles and saints. In the East, in the lands controlled by the Byzantine emperors, such religious-oriented artworks were called icons. A huge controversy over the icons erupted between 726 and 730 when the highly conservative Byzantine emperor Leo III denounced these images. He claimed that venerating an icon or other religious artwork was no different than worshipping a human-made image of God, which was forbidden in the Ten Commandments. So the existing icons should be destroyed, a view or position that came to be called iconoclasm. A number of people strongly disagreed, among them a Syrian monk named John of Damascus, the chief defender of the icons in the East, and Pope Gregory II, the main supporter of religious art in the West. The iconoclasts eventually lost the argument, and by the end of the ninth century the controversy was over. But in the meantime, thousands of magnificent mosaics and other early medieval artworks had been destroyed by religious fanatics.

Byzantine emperor Leo III became the first iconoclast when he denounced religious icons because they were human-made images of God, a practice forbidden by the second commandment.

for the most part, paintings, especially frescoes, came to be favored over mosaics in the West in the late medieval period. Among the few major mosaics produced in the late Middle Ages, two of the finest appeared during the Renaissance. One was a large work designed by Giotto for the atrium of the original Saint Peter's in Rome. The other was *The Creation of the World*, a splendid mosaic designed by another great painter, Raphael, for Rome's Chigi Chapel.

Colored Light from God

At the same time that mosaics were losing ground to frescoes in the Gothic period of medieval art, stained glass windows were gaining in popularity and spreading rapidly. Glass had been used extensively in Greco-Roman society and art. However, colored glass was used mostly in making vases and other sorts of portable glass items.

Among the first examples of colored, or stained, glass used for medieval church windows were an unknown number made in Britain in the late 600s. They have not survived, although archaeologists have found some assorted pieces of colored glass that they think were once part of them. Such special windows remained rare and scattered in Europe until the great burst of church building that instigated the Romanesque period shortly after 1000. Some stained glass windows were made in that era. But they did not become part of a major, widely practiced art form until the rise of the first Gothic cathedrals in the mid-1100s. An expert on medieval stained glass, the late Alfred Werck, explained one of the reasons that the Gothic years witnessed such a huge increase in the use of these windows:

> In the Romanesque period, the windows [of churches] were still relatively small, and the large wall spaces supplied room for the development of fresco paintings. A change came with the new architectural style [Gothic], which from the beginning made it possible to break up the wall space by distributing the weight of the arches and roof upon special parts of the wall supported by flying buttresses. The window space in Gothic architecture

thus makes a significant gain in width and height, and fresco paintings, left with insufficient space or no space at all, [gave way] to [stained] glass.[56]

The designer of the Gothic Basilica of Saint-Denis in Paris, Abbot Suger, was one of the first enthusiastic proponents of stained glass windows for churches. "In Suger's vision, light was the primary source of faith and divine inspiration,"[57] noted scholar Norman F. Cantor points out. According to this view, it was a spiritual light that came directly from God and fed the

Abbot Suger designed the stained glass windows in the Basilica of Saint-Denis in Paris to serve as a source of faith and inspiration.

COOKING THE COLORS

Early medieval glassmakers had a very difficult time preparing the colors they wanted to use in their stained glass panels. This was because the production of various colors was often the result of temperature differences that occurred while the glass was hot and in liquid form. In the book he wrote for craftsmen in about A.D. 1100, the monk Theophilus said:

If you notice a pot of melted glass turning yellow, let it boil for three hours and you will have a clear yellow. If you wish, let it boil for six hours and you will have a red-yellow. If you notice, however, that the pot is turning reddish, so that it resembles flesh, take [some of the glass] and use it for flesh color [in the window]. Boil the rest for two hours and you will have a bright purple, and another three hours, a real red-purple.

Quoted in Alfred Werck. *Stained Glass.* Charleston, SC: Nabu, 2010, pp. 75–76.

human soul. It was preferable, even necessary, therefore, to install windows in churches that would allow liberal amounts of light to flood the interiors of these structures. Yet it was no less important to dress that light in the finest religious array possible—which took the form of magnificent stained glass panels bearing biblical scenes.

To make such panels in the Gothic period, an artisan first cut a piece of wood so that it was identical in size with the window to come. He then sketched the desired scene on the wood, making sure to indicate the colors he wanted for various parts of the picture. Next, a glassblower created some sheets of glass, each a different color. From those sheets, the artisan cut out pieces and laid them on the wooden template in the appropriate places. When he was satisfied with the layout, he joined the pieces together with narrow lead strips called cames. Finally, he lifted the completed window off the wood and placed it in a pre-assembled iron frame in the window opening.

Among the most ambitious and beautiful series of Gothic stained glass windows was that installed in stages in Chartres Cathedral between 1210 and 1260. In all, roughly 22,000 square feet (2,046 sq. m) of glass were installed. The great cathedral at Reims (80 miles, or 129 kilometers, northeast of Paris), erected in the same decades as Chartres, was and remains famous for its rose windows. A rose window is a special round variety of stained glass window in which the glass panels are framed by thin stone strips called mullions. The two examples on the west end of the Reims cathedral, one of which shows the Virgin Mary's death and resurrection, are widely viewed to be among the great masterpieces of medieval art. Still awe-inspiring in their complexity and beauty, they recall the European world of a bygone age. It was in that era, one modern expert comments, that great glimmers of glorious color first "streamed into places of worship all across Europe, bringing light and meaning to the promise of eternal enlightenment from heaven."[58]

Tapestry, Jewelry, and Other Fine Crafts

Medieval European society boasted numerous talented artisans who worked in a wide variety of traditional crafts and turned out finely made products worthy of calling art. They included goldsmiths, silversmiths, and other metalworkers; cabinetmakers and other furniture makers; jewelers; makers of glassware and ceramic tableware; ivory carvers; porcelain makers; makers of enamel (glass fused to metal); embroiderers and tapestry makers; and sword and armor makers, among others. At least a few examples of works from each of these crafts have survived. They attest to the time, care, and attention to detail invested in their creation and thereby to the pride and dedication of the artists.

Embroidery

Embroidery is the textile art of decorating fabric by sewing colored threads or yarns onto existing fabric. The decorations can consist of patterned borders featuring repeated geometric shapes or abstract designs, or in more complex examples, pictorial scenes. Examples of carefully made, attractive embroidery made in the Middle Ages have been found in sites across Europe. Among the oldest and finest are from England, which early on became known for its high-quality embroidery.

English-made embroidery, the most popular and coveted needlework in medieval times, was known as *opus anglicanum,* or "English work."

The earliest surviving examples (not only from England but from all of Europe) are the Maaseik embroideries, named after the town in Belgium where they are now displayed. Remnant's of a churchman's vestment, or outfit, they were made somewhere in England in the late 800s. The threads, which are of silk dyed beige, red, yellow, green and blue, form repeated decorations featuring geometric patterns, foliage, and animals.

In the centuries that followed, English embroidery competed in European markets with works made in other countries but continued to be the most popular and coveted. By the 1200s the English variety, which had come to be called *opus anglicanum*, was in great demand. To keep up with this demand, large workshops arose, most often in the commercial districts of large towns. According to Jane Stockton, an expert on medieval embroidery:

> High quality English embroidery was made of expensive imported materials and was very labor intensive. Nuns and noblewomen did a great deal of embroidery as one would expect, but large embroideries . . . were made by highly trained professionals, both men and women. They were employed in workshops which were funded by merchants and noble patrons. It was the

merchants who took the profits, not the embroiderers, who received only modest payments for their work. Most workshops were in London where the necessary capital [financial backing] was available and which was the principal port through which the imported materials arrived.[59]

One of the finest surviving examples of late medieval embroidery from outside of England comes from Heiningen, Germany. Made in 1516, it is a wall hanging that measures almost 264 square feet (24.5 sq. m) and depicts in extraordinary detail a prim, well-dressed woman (representing the intellectual discipline of philosophy) surrounded by twenty-three other human figures. This work is also noteworthy because all of the fifty-eight nuns who worked on it, along with their prioress, signed it.

SPLENDID EMBROIDERY BY GERMAN NUNS

The large embroidered wall hanging from Heiningen, Germany, made by nuns in 1516, is among the finest surviving examples of this kind of artwork from late medieval Europe. British Museum scholar Norbert Jopek describes the work's complex imagery:

The seated figure of Philosophy [rests] in the center, surrounded by five smaller figures representing the branches of philosophical learning: theory, logic, practical science, mechanical science, and physics. An outer ring shows the figures of the seven Liberal Arts alternating with the Virtues and the gifts of the Holy Spirit. The seated men in the corners represent the four wise men of Antiquity [ancient times]: Ovid, Boethius, Horace, and Aristotle.

Norbert Jopek. "Labor and Meditation: A Convent Embroidery." In *Medieval and Renaissance Art: People and Possessions*, by Glyn Davies and Kirstin Kennedy. London: V & A, 2009, p. 78.

Tapestries

The largest and most impressive of all the medieval embroideries is the so-called Bayeux Tapestry. Here the word *tapestry* is a misnomer, as the piece was clearly embroidered by hand. (A tapestry is a work of textile art that is made on a vertical loom. In contrast to embroidery, in which the images are sewn into existing fabric, in a tapestry the images are created while the fabric itself is woven on the loom.) Made in England, the Bayeux Tapestry is 231 feet (70.4m) long and about 20 inches (50cm) high, and it tells in fifty-eight separate scenes the story of the Norman invasion of England in 1066. Janetta Benton describes the distinctive storytelling approach employed in it and other large-scale works of medieval textile art:

> The entire Bayeux Tapestry is laid out like a medieval prototype for today's comic strips, with a series of scenes in chronological sequence. [Although] there are no firm divisions between the scenes, the viewer can readily see where one ends and the next begins. Many shorthand devices are used to facilitate telling the tale. In this abbreviated form of narrative, an entire city can be reduced to a theater prop and settings are only as detailed as required to indicate where an event takes place. Figures are shown inside of a building by removing a wall to allow visual access to the interior, which is drawn without benefit to perspective. The entire work is conceived as flat areas of color within firm dark outlines, much like contemporary murals.[60]

Although the Bayeux Tapestry is technically not a tapestry, it does resemble some of the real tapestries made in the same period. The tapestry art form dates back to the Hellenistic Age, the highly productive period of ancient Greek culture that followed the death of Alexander the Great in 323 B.C. But tapestries did not come to be made in large numbers in medieval Europe until the 1300s and 1400s. In the words of New York Metropolitan Museum of Art scholar Thomas P. Campbell:

Tapestries were ubiquitous [seen everywhere] in the castles and churches of the late medieval and Renaissance eras. At a practical level, they provided a form of insulation [to keep cold out] and decoration that could be easily transported. . . . Many medieval tapestries measure as much as 5 x 10 yards and sets could include ten or more pieces. While much production was relatively coarse, intended for decorative purposes, wealthy patrons could commission designs whose subjects embodied celebratory or propagandistic themes. Enriched with silk and gilt metallic thread, such tapestries were a central component of the ostentatious [showy] magnificence used by powerful secular and religious rulers to broadcast their wealth and might.[61]

The Bayeux Tapestry is 231 feet long and 20 inches high. In fifty-eight different scenes it depicts the story of the invasion of England in 1066.

Some of the more famous and artistically complex surviving late medieval tapestries are *The Lady and the Unicorn*, in six sections, made in Flanders (now Belgium, France, and the Netherlands) in the late 1500s; *The Story of the Trojan War*, woven in the Netherlands between 1470 and 1490; and *The Acts of the Apostles*, made in Belgium in the early 1500s. The latter work, made up of ten sections, was commissioned by Pope Leo X for the Sistine Chapel in the Vatican. This tapestry

Woven in the Netherlands between 1470 and 1490, *The Story of the Trojan War* is a fine example of the complexities of late medieval tapestries.

is further significant because the original drawings (called "cartoons") on which it was based were created by the great Renaissance painter Raphael and have survived.

Monumental Metalwork

In the same years that these large tapestries were in production, European metalworkers were creating some outstanding monumental bronze statues, which were commissioned by both churches and nobles. Moderate-sized metal artworks had

Donatello's sculpture *Gattamelata*, created between 1444 and 1453, was the first large equestrian statue to be created since the fall of Rome.

been made in earlier centuries, notably some in the Romanesque and Gothic periods. For example, a magnificent copper candlestick was made for Saint Peter's Church (now Gloucester Cathedral) in southwestern England in the early 1100s. Standing 23 inches (58cm) high, it now rests in London's Victoria and Albert Museum. Dating from a bit more than two centuries later is the *Virgin and Child* from the Gothic Basilica of Saint-Denis, not far north of Paris. Slightly more than 2 feet (69cm) high, it is a silver gilt (silver coated with gold) piece depicting Mary holding the baby Jesus.

Considerably larger and more elaborate and dramatic were a number of metal statues made during the Renaissance. It has been established that Donatello's *David*, a life-size bronze figure, was the first large nude statue made in Europe since ancient times. Donatello also created a life-size bronze equestrian statue—that is, a rendering of a person mounted on a horse—between 1444 and 1453. It was the first large equestrian statue produced since Rome's fall, and it still stands in the Piazza del Santo in Padua. Its title, *Gattamelata*, was the nickname of the renowned fifteenth-century Italian mercenary soldier Erasmo of Narni, whom Donatello depicted on the horse. People from all parts of Europe journeyed to Padua to see this great artwork. Not surprisingly, it inspired the manufacture of many similar equestrian statues of military heroes in the following three centuries.

To make large metal artworks like the *Gattamelata*, Donatello and other Renaissance artists typically employed the lost wax method, which was pioneered by the ancient Greeks. The first step was to acquire large amounts of modeling clay and with it fashion a full-size model of the proposed statue. (To keep it from sagging or collapsing, the clay was supported by an iron framework.) In the next step, the artist and his assistants placed the model in a large oven and baked it until it was hard. Then they coated it with a thick layer of wax and poured wet plaster around it (or covered it with more clay). In the next step, they heated the mold, causing the wax to melt and drain away through a small hole in the bottom. That left a matrix, or hollow space, between the original model and the plaster or clay outer layer. Into the matrix they poured liquid bronze and waited until the metal had completely hardened. Chipping away the plaster or clay, they gazed on the finished hollow bronze statue.

One of the greatest metal artworks made this way during the late Renaissance was the *Perseus and Medusa* of Florentine metalsmith Benvenuto Cellini (born 1500). Standing 18 feet (5.5m) tall, the statue portrays the mythical Greek hero Perseus holding the severed head of the hideous monster Medusa (known for having snakes for hair). In his well-known autobiography, Cellini recalled the moment when the huge, majestic work was revealed to the public, saying, "A shout of boundless enthusiasm went up in commendation of my work, which consoled me not a little. The folk kept on [writing poems], all of them overflowing with the highest [praises]. And all the doctors and scholars [from a nearby university] kept vying with each other [over] who could praise it best."[62]

Florentine metalsmith Benvenuto Cellini's *Perseus and Medusa* is one of the great metalworks of the late Renaissance era.

ARTISTIC TALENT GOD'S GIFT?

A fair amount of what is known today about medieval craft workers and artists and their methods comes from a treatise titled On Diverse Arts. *It was written in about 1125 by a German monk, metalworker, and builder named Roger of Helmarshausen, who used the pseudonym Theophilus. In this excerpt from the preface of his book, Theophilus presents his view that artistic talent is a gift bestowed on humans by God in a master plan designed to glorify the deity's image.*

In the account of the creation of the world, we read that man was created in the image and likeness of God and was animated by the Divine breath, breathed into him. By the eminence of such distinction, he was placed above the other living creatures, so that, capable of reason, he acquired participation in the wisdom and skill of the Divine Intelligence, and . . . transmitted to later posterity the distinction of wisdom and intelligence, that whoever will contribute both care and concern is able to attain a capacity for all arts and skills, as if by hereditary right. Human skill sustained this purpose and, in its various activities, pursued profit and pleasure and, finally, with the passage of time transmitted it to the predestined age of Christian religion. So, it has come about that, what God intended to create for the praise and glory of His name, a people devoted to God has restored to His worship.

Medieval Sourcebook. "Theophilus: An Essay Upon Diverse Arts." www.fordham.edu/halsall/source/theophilus.html.

Jewelry Fit for a King

Various kinds of metal appeared on a smaller scale in another craftsman's fine art popular in the Middle Ages—jewelry making. In the early medieval centuries, jewelry was both widespread and important among the non-Christian Germanic peoples who occupied large swaths of central and northern Europe and Britain. Most examples of jewelry from the period, including finely made brooches (to fasten dresses or cloaks) and buckles, were found in graves of persons from the upper classes, who in one scholar's words "were buried fully dressed and bejeweled." She adds, "This custom continued into the Christian period [the seventh and eighth centuries onward] and demonstrates that the manner of burial reflected status as well as faith."[63] Indeed, it appears that the more elaborate and expensive the brooch, the higher the social status of the wearer. The most common materials used in such brooches were silver, gold, garnet, semiprecious stones, glass, brass, Mediterranean sea shells, and bronze.

Using jewelry as an indicator of wealth and/or social status and rank continued in the later medieval centuries across Europe. In some areas it was frowned on for anyone having a lower social rank than a knight to wear expensive jewelry. In fact, numerous European towns passed laws to maintain this firm line between nobles and common folk.

The variety of jewelry forms and items was greater in the later medieval period than it had been earlier. Both men and women wore rings, brooches, chains bearing medallions, girdles (wide belts worn diagonally across the torso), and chaplets (strings of prayer beads). The materials used to fashion these items included, among others, gold, silver, ivory, pearls, sapphires, rubies, enamel, quartz, glass, and bronze.

The most impressive jewelry artworks were those that combined many of these materials in one item. Perhaps the most stunning examples of all were the crowns worn by Europe's monarchs over the medieval centuries. Many of these have not survived. But one that still exists gives a clear idea of how beautiful and priceless they were. The crown in question was worn by several of the later Holy Roman emperors (the German rulers who succeeded Charlemagne's Frankish family in the tenth and eleventh centuries), including Otto I and Conrad II. It features 144 precious stones, including emeralds, sapphires, and amethysts, and roughly the same number of large pearls. All are set into a series of eight interconnected plates made of 22-carat gold. Some of the plates also bear scenes from the Bible rendered in enamel and surrounded by

blue sapphires. In addition, a gem-studded Christian cross rises prominently from the crown's top-front portion. This magnificent piece, a true example of jewelry fit for a king, is on display in the Hofburg Palace in Vienna, Austria. (An identical copy can be seen in the town hall at Aachen, once Charlemagne's capital.)

The Hofburg crown, Cellini's *Perseus*, Donatello's *Gattamelata*, the Bayeux Tapestry, the *Mona Lisa*, Giotto's paintings, the grand cathedrals at Chartres and Reims, the quirky

The Hofburg crown was worn by several Holy Roman emperors and is made of gold and precious stones.

HOLY ROBBERY!

*A*mong the finest creations of medieval artist-craftspeople were reliquaries—containers that held sacred relics, including bones, skulls, hairs, toenails, and other body parts of deceased saints and other religious figures. Relics were seen as so holy and valuable that on occasion monks stole them in order to acquire them for their own churches. Such acts became known as "holy robbery." In the 800s, for example, a group of monks from the abbey-church at Conques in southern France swiped the skull of Saint Foy (or Saint Faith) from a shrine in a neighboring region. They used the excuse that the saint had urged them to do the deed because she strongly desired her remains to rest in their church. The holy robbers placed the skull inside a statue (of the saint sitting on a throne) made of gold and studded with numerous precious gems. This magnificent reliquary is now on display in the cathedral at Conques.

entranceway to the Laurentian Library, and thousands of other splendid surviving masterpieces of medieval art are more popular today than they were when they were first made. At first glance this may seem odd or illogical. But the fact is that each year, tens of thousands (and in some cases hundreds of thousands) of tourists travel long distances to see them. For sheer beauty they are marvels to behold, indeed. Yet it is the genius and unwavering diligence of their creators that makes them compelling artworks for the ages. As Benton aptly puts it, it is "a testimony to the ability and accomplishment of medieval artists that even today—so very many years later—[their] works] are still providing visitors with pleasure."[64]

Notes

Introduction: For the Glory of God

1. Dante Alighieri. *The Divine Comedy*. Canto 11:105. Translated by Henry Wadsworth Longfellow. Electronic Literature Foundation. www.divine comedy.org/divine_comedy.html.
2. Anne Fremantle. *Age of Faith*. New York: Time-Life, 1979, p. 117.
3. Glyn Davies and Kirstin Kennedy. *Medieval and Renaissance Art: People and Possessions*. London: V & A, 2009, p. 63.
4. Janetta R. Benton. *The Art of the Middle Ages*. London: Thames and Hudson, 2002, pp. 17–18.
5. Benton. *The Art of the Middle Ages*, p. 17.
6. Quoted in Marjorie Rowling. *Life in Medieval Times*. New York: Berkeley, 1987, p. 156.
7. Quoted in Rowling. *Life in Medieval Times*, p. 157.
8. Benton. *The Art of the Middle Ages*, p. 18.
9. Fremantle. *Age of Faith*, p. 126.

Chapter 1: Castles and Other Secular Architecture

10. Judith M. Bennett and C. Warren Hollister. *Medieval Europe: A Short History*. Boston: McGraw-Hill, 2006, p. 300.
11. Benton. *The Art of the Middle Ages*, p. 19.
12. Nicola Coldstream. *Medieval Architecture*. New York: Oxford University Press, 2002, p. 29.
13. Marilyn Stokstad. *Art: A Brief History*. Upper Saddle River, NJ: Pearson, 2009, p. 272.
14. Coldstream. *Medieval Architecture*, p. 168.
15. Coldstream. *Medieval Architecture*, p. 171.
16. Roy Bolton. *A Brief History of Painting*. London: Magpie, 2004, p. 19.
17. Stokstad. *Art*, p. 288.
18. Michael Raeburn. *Architecture of the World*. New York: Galahad, 1975, p. 56.
19. Elke Linda Buchholz et al. *Art: A World History*. New York: Abrams, 2007, p. 150.
20. Giorgio Vasari. *Lives of the Most Eminent Painters, Sculptors and Architects*. Vol. 5. London: Henry G. Bohn, 1912, p. 272.

Chapter 2: Churches and Other Religious Structures

21. Stokstad. *Art*, p. 232.
22. Charles Freeman. *The World of the Romans*. New York: Oxford University Press, 1995, p. 162.
23. Einhard. *Life of Charlemagne*. Excerpted in *The Medieval Reader*, by Norman F. Cantor. New York: HarperCollins, 1994, p. 102.
24. Stokstad. *Art*, p. 237.
25. Quoted in Elizabeth G. Holt, ed. *Literary Sources of Art History*. Princeton, NJ: Princeton University Press, 1947, p. 3.
26. Holly Haynes. "Basilica of St. Sernin, Toulouse." Sacred Destinations. www.sacred-destinations.com/france/toulouse-st-sernin.
27. Coldstream. *Medieval Architecture*, p. 97.
28. Stokstad. *Art*, p. 256.
29. Rowling. *Life in Medieval Times*, p. 170.
30. Quoted in James Neal. *Architecture: A Visual History*. New York: Sterling, 2001, p. 17.

Chapter 3: Sculpture: Romanesque to Renaissance

31. James Snyder. *Medieval Art: Painting, Sculpture, Architecture, 4th–14th Century*. Englewood Cliffs, NJ: Prentice-Hall, 2006, p. 95.
32. Stokstad. *Art*, p. 249.
33. Stokstad. *Art*, p. 250.
34. Uwe Geese. "Gothic Sculpture in France, Italy, Germany, and England." In *Gothic: Architecture, Sculpture, Painting*, edited by Rolf Toman. Cologne, Germany: Tandem Verlag, 2007, p. 321.
35. John Haber. "The Gates to the City." *Haber Arts.com*. www.haberarts.com/ghiberti.htm.
36. Buchholz. *Art: A World History*, pp. 128–129.
37. Quoted in J.A. Symonds. *Life of Michelangelo Buonarroti*. Philadelphia: University of Pennsylvania Press, 2002, p. 70.
38. Benvenuto Cellini. *The Treatises of Benvenuto Cellini on Goldsmithing and Sculpture*. Translated by C.R. Ashbee. New York: Dover, 1967, p. 144.

Chapter 4: Evolving Painting Forms and Techniques

39. Bolton. *A Brief History of Painting*, p. 18.
40. Susanne Kaeppele. "Late Antiquity and the Middle Ages." In *Art: A World History*, p. 83.
41. Enrico Annosica et al. *Art: A World History*. London: Dorling Kindersley, 1999, p. 147.
42. Cennino Cennini. *Il Libro dell'Arte*. Translated by Daniel V. Thompson Jr. New York: Dover, 1933, pp. 41–43.
43. Kaeppele. "Late Antiquity and the Middle Ages," p. 94.
44. Quoted in Elizabeth G. Holt, ed. *A Documentary History of Art*. New Haven, CT: Yale University Press, 1986, p. 69.

45. Bolton. *A Brief History of Painting*, p. 22.

46. Giorgio Vasari. *Lives of the Most Eminent Painters, Sculptors and Architects*. Vol. 1. Translated by Gaston de Vere. London: Macmillan, 1912, pp. 71–72, 84.

47. Stokstad. *Art*, p. 283.

48. Kaeppele. "Late Antiquity and the Middle Ages," p. 110.

49. Charles L. Mee Jr. *Daily Life in Renaissance Italy*. New York: American Heritage, 1975, p. 92.

50. Bolton. *A Brief History of Painting*, p. 48.

51. Mee. *Daily Life in Renaissance Italy*, p. 92.

52. Buchholz. *Art: A World History*, p. 154.

53. Giorgio Vasari. *Lives of the Most Eminent Painters, Sculptors and Architects*. Vol. 9. Translated by Gaston de Vere. London: Macmillan, 1912, p. 33.

Chapter 5: Mosaics and Stained Glass: A Dual Role

54. Stokstad. *Art*, p. 174.

55. Benton. *The Art of the Middle Ages*, pp. 29–30.

56. Alfred Werck. *Stained Glass*. Charleston, SC: Nabu, 2010, pp. 50–51.

57. Norman F. Cantor, ed. *The Encyclopedia of the Middle Ages*. New York: Viking, 1999, p. 398.

58. Annosica. *Art: A World History*, p. 197.

Chapter 6: Tapestry, Jewelry, and Other Fine Crafts

59. Jane Stockton. "Opus Anglicanum." Historical Needlework Resources. http://medieval.webcon.net.au/technique_opus_anglicanum.html.

60. Benton. *The Art of the Middle Ages*, pp. 101–103.

61. Thomas P. Campbell. "European Tapestry Production and Patronage, 1400–1600." New York Metropolitan Museum of Art. www.metmuseum.org/ toah/hd/taps/hd_ taps.htm.

62. Benvenuto Cellini. *Autobiography*. Translated by John A. Symonds. Charleston, SC: Nabu, 2010, p. 500.

63. Sonja Marzinzik. "German Jewelry of the Early Middle Ages: Status, Beauty, Artistry." In *Medieval and Renaissance Art*, p. 74.

64. Benton. *The Art of the Middle Ages*, p. 301.

Glossary

aesthetic: Relating to emotions, feelings, and/or artistic impulses.

altarpiece: An artwork that decorates a church's altar.

antiquity: Ancient times.

apse: A semicircular chamber extending from one or both ends of a basilica.

arch: An architectural form, usually shaped like a semicircle, used to span the top of a door, window, bridge support, or other open space.

archivolts: The moldings following the curve of the arch above the tympanum in a Christian church.

bailey: In medieval Europe, a courtyard, usually enclosed by a defensive wall.

barrel vault: A corridor having a curved ceiling.

basilica: A Roman building with a large, high-ceilinged central space, used for court trials and public meetings; in medieval Europe, a church based on the basilica form.

Biblia pauperum: "Poor people's Bible"; artistic forms, notably painting, sculpture, mosaics, and stained glass, that were used to tell biblical stories to illiterate worshippers in medieval churches.

bronze: A metal alloy made by mixing copper and tin.

cames: The lead strips joining together the individual pieces of glass in a stained glass window.

capital: The topmost section of a column.

chaplet: A string of prayer beads.

classical: Greco-Roman.

coffering: Sunken or recessed areas of wooden or stone panels, most often in ceilings.

colonnade: A row of columns.

crenellation: The notched effect in the battlements of forts, castles, and other ancient and medieval structures.

diptych: A decorative object having two carved panels connected by a hinge.

drawbridge: A movable wooden platform spanning a moat in front of a castle's main gate.

embroidery: A textile art in which images are sewn into an existing piece of fabric.

enamel: In medieval Europe, glass fused to metal.

evangelists: The anonymous writers of the four biblical Gospels, traditionally represented by the names Matthew, Mark, Luke, and John.

facade: The outward front section of a building.

flying buttress: A partial stone arch on a building's side that lends support to the structure's upper sections.

fresco: A painting done on wet plaster.

girdle: In medieval Europe, a wide belt worn diagonally across the chest.

hall: The principal chamber in the living quarters of a medieval castle or house.

illuminated manuscript: In the Middle Ages, an illustrated Bible or other book.

machicolation: The outward projection of a wall at the top of the battlement of a fort or castle.

masonry: Stone or brick.

master builder (or master mason): In medieval times, a combination of architect, building contractor, and general overseer.

monumental: Large-scale.

motte: In medieval Europe, an earthen mound on which early castles were built.

nave: The large, open space in the center of a basilica.

order: An architectural style, usually identified by the main features of its columns, including the Doric, Ionic, and Corinthian orders.

panel painting: A painting done on a piece of wood; or the art of painting on wood.

pilaster: An architectural decoration consisting of a partial or flattened column that projects only slightly from a wall.

portal sculptures: Carvings located above and around the main entrances of Christian churches.

relic: A bone, skull, piece of clothing, or other object that once belonged to a saint or other past religious figure.

reliefs (or bas-reliefs): Sculpted images or scenes in which the figures and/or objects depicted are raised from, but still attached to, a flat surface.

reliquary: A container for relics.

rose window: A round stained glass window.

scriptorium: A workroom, usually in a monastery or convent, where illustrated manuscripts were made.

secco: The technique of painting on dry plaster.

secular: Nonreligious.

tapestry: A textile art in which images are created on fabric as it is woven on a loom.

tesserae: Individual cubes or tiles used to make mosaics.

tracery: Delicately interlaced lines.

trumeau: The supporting post located between the double front doors of a building.

turret: A small tower.

tympanum: The hemispherical area located within an arch that is directly above the front doors of a building.

westwork: A stone tower built into the front of a Christian church.

For More Information

Books

Enrico Annosica et al. *Art: A World History*. London: Dorling Kindersley, 1999. One of the better general overviews of art history available, this volume contains numerous reproductions of important examples of painting, sculptures, architecture, and other art forms through the ages.

James Barter. *In the Glory of God: Medieval Art*. Farmington Hills, MI: Lucent, 2006. This excellent volume aimed at junior high and high school students contains well-researched overviews of the major medieval art forms.

Janetta R. Benton. *The Art of the Middle Ages*. London: Thames and Hudson, 2002. Benton delivers a well-rounded study of medieval art, with special emphasis placed on regional styles and achievements.

Roy Bolton. *A Brief History of Painting*. London: Magpie, 2004. A noted British art historian, Bolton tells how painting developed over the centuries in clear, concise prose supported by numerous beautiful reproductions of paintings.

Elke Linda Buchholz et al. *Art: A World History*. New York: Abrams, 2007. Written in an easy-to-read style, this handsomely mounted book features two or more photos of major artworks on every page.

Francis D.K. Ching et al. *A Global History of Architecture*. New York: Wiley, 2006. This ambitious volume presents a comprehensive overview of architecture through the ages in all parts of the world.

Nicola Coldstream. *Medieval Architecture*. New York: Oxford University Press, 2002. A straightforward treatment of the subject, this book features numerous stunning photos of artworks, as well as helpful diagrams of art forms.

Glyn Davies and Kirstin Kennedy. *Medieval and Renaissance Art: People and Possessions*. London: V & A, 2009. The authors, who are museum curators, have created an easy-to-understand introduction to all areas of artistic production in the Middle Ages and Renaissance.

Steven S. Delaware et al. *Art and Culture of the Medieval World*. New York:

Rosen, 2010. Written for young people, this is a colorfully illustrated introduction to the topic.

David Franklin, ed. *Leonardo da Vinci, Michelangelo, and the Renaissance in Florence*. New Haven, CT: Yale University Press, 2005. The editor has compiled a collection of useful expert observations of the works of these two great artistic masters.

H.W. Janson and Anthony F. Janson. *History of Art*. New York: Abrams, 1997. This major study of art history contains large amounts of information about the evolution of the various art forms and features numerous beautiful illustrations of examples of each form.

J.E. Kaufman et al. *The Medieval Fortress: Castles, Forts, and Walled Cities of the Middle Ages*. New York: Da Capo, 2004. The book offers a synopsis of medieval architecture and building techniques, along with information about how medieval structures were used.

John Mills. *Encyclopedia of Sculpture Techniques*. London: Batsford, 2005. This unusual and beautifully mounted book provides a great deal of data on the specific methods employed by sculptors of the past and present.

Lauren Murphy and Rupert Matthews. *Art and Culture of the Renaissance World*. New York: Rosen, 2010. Filled with attractive illustrations showing Renaissance art treasures, this children's book provides a general overview of architecture, painting, and sculpture in that important period.

James Snyder. *Medieval Art: Painting, Sculpture, Architecture, 4th–14th Century*. Englewood Cliffs, NJ: Prentice-Hall, 2006. This is one of the better recent attempts to summarize a huge, complex subject. The inclusion of floor plans of several churches and other structures is helpful.

Marilyn Stokstad. *Art: A Brief History*. Upper Saddle River, NJ: Pearson, 2009. The combination of straightforward, authoritative writing and superior presentation makes this one of the best available books on art history.

Rolf Toman, ed. *Gothic: Architecture, Sculpture, Painting*. Cologne, Germany: Tandem Verlag, 2007. Several leading experts explain and discuss Gothic art in this visually splendid volume.

Rolf Toman, ed. *Romanesque: Architecture, Sculpture, Painting*. Cologne, Germany: Konemann, 1997. A companion book to Toman's study of Gothic art, this book is magnificently mounted.

Sidney Toy. *Castles: Their Construction and History*. New York: Dover, 1985. An expert on historical fortifications delivers one of the classic studies of castle construction and the cultural effects of these vital medieval structures.

Websites

"The Bayeux Tapestry," Australian National University (http://rubens.anu.edu.au/htdocs/bytype/textiles/bayeux). This site contains photos of all the separate scenes of the famous tapestry. Clicking on a scene brings up a larger view of it.

"Castles," Medieval Plus.com (www.medievalplus.com/castles). This colorful site provides an easy-to-read synopsis of medieval castles and their features.

"Donatello," Metropolitan Museum of Art (www.metmuseum.org/toah/hd/dona/hd_dona.htm). A brief but authoritative overview of this great Renaissance artist and his works.

"Michelangelo Buonarroti," Neil R. Bonner (www.michelangelo.com/buonarroti.html). The home page of an excellent series of websites devoted to the life and works of one of the greatest sculptors who ever lived. Contains many stunning photos of his sculptures, paintings, and architectural achievements.

"Romanesque Architecture," Digital Archive of Architecture (www.bc.edu/bc_org/avp/cas/fnart/arch/romanesque_arch.html). Click on the individual photos of Romanesque buildings in this well-organized site to enlarge them.

Index

A

Alberti, Leon Battista, 21, 22, 24
The Album of Villard de Honnecourt (Honnecourt), *37*
Apprentice painters, 57, 61, 64
Architecture, 14
  classical, 20, 22
  focus on inner spaces of, 22–24
  of Michelangelo, 26–27
  relationship between sculpture and, 47–49
  secular, 15–19
Artists
  anonymity of, 13
  divine inspiration of, 95
  religious restrictions on, 11–13

B

Basilica of Saint Lawrence (San Lorenzo, Florence), 41
Basilica of Saint Mary of the Flowers (Florence), dome of (Brunelleschi), *39,* 40–41
Basilica of Saint-Denis (Paris), 17, 38, 42, 92
  stained glass windows of, *82,* 82–83
Baths of Caracalla (Rome), 23
Bayeux Tapestry, 88, *89*
Bellano, Bartolomeo, 57
Bellini, Giovanni, 61

Bennett, Judith M., 15
Benton, Janetta R., 11, 76, 88, 98
Bernini, Gian Lorenzo, 43
Biblica pauperum, 73
Boccaccio, Giovanni, 21
Bolton, Roy, 20, 58–59, 70
Bondone, Giotto di, 10. *See* Giotto di Bondone
Botticelli, Sandro, 70
Brunelleschi, Filippo, 25, 39, 40–41
Buchholz, Elke Linda, 26, 54–55, 71
Buoninsegna, Duccio di. *See* Duccio di Buoninsegna
Byzantine art, *59*
  influence on Western art, 62, 67, 76
  mosaics, 75
  paintings, 58–59
Byzantine Empire, 29

C

Campbell, Thomas P., 88–89
Campidoglio (Rome), 26
Cantor, Norman F., 82
Castles
  artistic features of, 19
  evolution of, 16–18
  motte-and-bailey, 17–18, *18*
  visual appeal of, 15–16
Cathedral of Saint Lazare (Autun, France), 49

tympanum of, 47–48, *48*
Catholic Church, 12
Cellini, Benvenuto, 57
  Perseus and Medusa, *94*
Cennini, Cennino, 64, 65
Charlemagne (Frankish king), 30, 33, 62
Charterhouse of Champmol (France), 50
Chartres Cathedral (France), 84
Church of Orsanmichele (Florence), 54
Church of San Vitale (Ravenna, Italy), mosaics in, *74, 76, 78*
Church of Santa Maria Maggiore (Rome), mosaics in, *74, 75*
Church of Santi Nereo e Achilleo (Rome), mosaic in, *78*
Churches/cathedrals
  early medieval, 30, 32
  Gothic, 35–36
  late Roman, 29
  Romanesque, 32–35
Cimabue (Cenni di Pepi), 66, 67–68
Coldstream, Nicola, 16, 19
  on master builders, 35
Columns, 40
  of Saint Peter's Basilica, 43
Constantine (Roman emperor), 74
The Creation of Adam (Michelangelo), 72
The Creation of the World (Raphael), 81
Crown, of Holy Roman emperors (Hofburg crown), 96–97, *97*

D
David (Donnatello), 54–55, 93
David (Michelangelo), 55, *56*

Davies, Glyn, 9–10
Delorme, Philibert, 26
Diptychs, 46
The Divine Comedy (Dante), 8
Dome, of Basilica of Saint Mary (Brunelleschi), *39*, 40–41
Donnatello (Donato di Niccolo di Betto Bardi), 52, 54, 92, 93
Duccio di Buoninsegna, 66, 67

E
Einhard, 30
Embroidery, 85–87
Erasmus, Desiderius, 21

F
Florence Baptistery, bronze doors of (Ghiberti), 51–52, 53, *53*
Flying buttresses, 36, *36*, 38
Fontana, Domenico, 42
Freeman, Charles, 29
Fremantle, Anne, 8–9, 13
Frescoes, 22, 65
  of Giotto, *68*, 69

G
The Gates of Paradise (Ghiberti), 52
Gattamelata (Donnatello), 92, 93
Ghiberti, Lorenzo, 53, 57
Giotto di Bondone, 66, 68, 81
Gislebertus (French artist), 49
Glaber, Raul, 32–33
Glassmaking, 83
Gothic period
  cathedrals, 35–36, 38
  panel paintings, 65–68
  sculptures, 49–51

stained glass windows, 81–84
Gregory II (pope), 80

H

Haber, John, 52
Hagia Sophia (Istanbul), 29, *31*
Heiningen, Germany, embroidered wall hanging of, 87
Hofburg crown, 96–97, *97*
Holy robbery, 98
Honnecourt, Villard de, 37
Humanists, 20, 21, 22

I

Iconoclasm, 80
Icons, Byzantine, 58–59, *59*
Illuminated manuscripts, 59, *60*, 60–62

J

Jewelry, 95–97
John of Damascus, 80
"John the Evangelist" (Lorsch Gospels), 62
Jones, Inigo, 26
Jopek, Norbert, 87
Justinian (Byzantine emperor), 76

K

Kaeppele, Susanne, 61–62, 65
Kennedy, Kirstin, 9–10

L

The Lady and the Unicorn tapestry, *90*
The Last Judgment (Cathedral of Saint Lazare), *48*
Last Supper (Leonardo di Vinci), 70
Leonardo di Vinci, 70, 71

Lindisfarne Gospels, *60*, 61–62
Lippi, Fra Filippo, 70
Lorsch Gospels, 46, 62
Lubow, Arthur, 53

M

Machicolation, 18
Madonna Enthroned (Bondone), *10*
Madonna with Child (Donnatello), *54*
Maesta Altarpiece (Duccio), 66, *67*
Malles Vendosta (Italy), mural in, *63*
Mantegna, Andrea, 70
Master builders, 32, 34–35
Mausoleum of Galla Placidia (Ravenna, Italy), 75
Maximianus (archbishop of Revenue), 46
Mee, Charles L., 70
Mentorship, 57, 64
Metalwork, monumental, 91–95, *92*, *94*
Michelangelo Buonarroti
  architectural work of, 26–27
  David, 56
  in design of Saint Peter's Basilica, 42
  paintings of, 72
  Piazza Campidoglio, *25*
  sculptures by, 55, 57
Middle Ages, definition of, 8
Mona Lisa (Leonardo di Vinci), 70
More, Thomas, 21, *21*
Mosaics, 73
  in Church of San Vitale, 76–77, *77*, *78*
  in Church of Santa Maria Maggiore, *74*
  in Church of Santi Nereo e Achilleo, *78*

early Christian, 74–75
early medieval, 75–78
late medieval, 78–79, 81
Motte-and-bailey castles, 17–18, *18*
Murals, 62, *63,* 64–65

N
Notre Dame Cathedral (Paris), 36, 38

O
Oil paints, 61

P
Paintings
 Gothic panel, 65–68
 of Michelangelo, 72
 realism in, 68–70, 68–72
 sculpture *vs.*, 9–10
 See also Frescoes
Palatine Chapel (Aachen, Germany),
 30
Palazzo Rucellai (Florence), 22
Palladio, Andrea, 25
Panel paintings, 65–68
The Parting of Lot and Abraham
 (Church of Santa Maria Maggiore),
 75
Perseus and Medusa (Cellini), 93–95, *94*
Petrarch, Francesco, 21
Philip the Bold, 50
Piazza Campidoglio (Michelangelo),
 25
Pietà (Michelangelo), 56
The Pillars of the Earth (Follett), 32
Pisano, Nicola, 49, 50
Poliziano (Italian scholar), 10
Porta, Giacomo della, 25, 42

R
Rabelais, François, 21
Raphael (Raphaello Sanzio), 70, 81
Realism, 70, 72
Reims cathedral (France), 84
Reliquaries, 46, 49, 98
Renaissance, 20
 architecture, 38, 40–43
 humanists of, 21
 paintings, 70, 72
 sculpture, 51–52, 54–55, 57
 spreads to northern Europe, 25–26
Roman Empire, disintegration of, 14
Roman mosaics, 74
Romanesque period
 carvings, 47–49
 churches, 32–35
 murals, 65
Romano, Giulio, 25

S
Saint Peter's Basilica (Rome), 29,
 41–43
Saint Peter's Church (England),
 copper candlestick of, 92
Saint-Sernin Basilica (Toulouse,
 France), 33–34, *34*
Scrovegni Chapel (Padua, Italy),
 frescoes of, *68,* 69
Sculpture
 early medieval, 44, 46–47
 Gothic, 49–51
 paintings *vs.*, debate over superiority
  of, 9–10
 Romanesque, 47–49
Secco, 65
Siena Cathedral

carved relief pulpit (Pisano), 49, 50
Maesta altarpiece in, *67*
Siena (Italy), town hall in, *20*
Sistine Chapel (Rome), 72
Sluter, Claus, 50–51
Snyder, James, 46–47
Stained glass, 73, 81–84
preparing colors for, 83
Stokstad, Marilyn, 19, 22, 28, 49, 69
The Story of the Trojan War tapestry, *91*
Suger (Abbot), 38, 42, 82

T
Tapestries, 88–91, *89, 90, 91*
Tempera, 61
Tesserae (tiles), 74, 77–78
Theodora (Byzantine empress), 76, 77, *77*
Theophilus, 83
Tidemann (German artisan), 12–13

Triptychs, 46

V
Van Eyck, Jan, 61
Vasari, Giorgio, 27, 69, 72
Virgil, 8
Virgin and Child (Basilica of Saint-Denis), 92
Virgin and Child Enthroned (Cimabue), 66
Virgin and Child Enthroned (Giotto), 66–67
Virgin and Child with St. Anne (Leonardo di Vinci), 71

W
Well of Moses (Sluter), 50–51
Werck, Alfred, 81–82
Westminster Hall (London), *23*, 23–24
William of Sens, 37

Picture Credits

About the Author

Historian Don Nardo is best known for his books for young people about the ancient and medieval worlds. These include volumes on the arts of ancient cultures, including Mesopotamian arts and literature, Egyptian sculpture and monuments, Greek temples, Roman amphitheaters, medieval castles, and general histories of sculpture, painting, and architecture through the ages. Nardo lives with his wife, Christine, in Massachusetts.